My Reading B...

My English Book Series

My Reading Book

My English Book Series

Authors

Barbara Hojel, M. S. Ed.   Arminda Chávez, Ph.D.

Consulting Reviewers

Monica Weddle
Macris Kindergarten
Tegucigalpa, Honduras

Beverly A. Wright
M. A. Ed. (ESL)
University of Kansas

ISBN: 0-673-19186-9

PREFACE

The publication of MY ENGLISH BOOK SERIES by Hojel and Chávez denotes a remarkable achievement. They have incorporated principles of learning developed and researched over the past forty years into a program for teaching English as a second language. In doing so, the authors have outlined a step-by-step program which provides teachers a road map for teaching and students a road map for learning English so that it becomes both a functional and meaningful means of communication.

The strength of the program lies in the fact that it provides the teacher with specific structured activities which, if followed, will ensure that the students in the program will learn. It does this by providing models for the student so that he or she will repeatedly hear examples of the English words to be learned in appropriate sentence structures. These are presented in such a way that it is easy for the child to associate the words with their meanings.

This is accomplished by providing the student with immediate and frequent opportunities to make both verbal and motor responses which indicate to the teacher that the child has understood the words modeled by the teacher. Furthermore, it provides for students to respond until they have achieved 100% accuracy in the basic use of English, a requirement necessary if a language is to become a functional tool of communication.

All too often, traditional approaches provide little opportunity for student responding. Often only one student makes a response at any one time, while most of the class sits without actively engaging in making learning responses. This program avoids that pitfall. The provision for all students to make many responses during each lesson also allows the teacher to provide frequent feedback, praise, and recognition for correct responses. Thus the program provides reinforcement for correct responding, an essential element for efficient learning.

If the authors had devised their program with no more than these elements (correct models, opportunity for frequent student responding, feedback, and reinforcement), the program would be superior to traditional approaches to teaching English as a second language. However, they have gone a step further. By arranging each year's lessons in a series of ten functional units, they have greatly increased the likelihood that the English the child learns will be functional and useful. That is, the students learn enough in each unit so that their grasp of language in that area allows them to communicate effectively. By learning enough of the sentence forms and vocabulary to converse in each of those unit areas, the student acquires the language tools needed for real communication rather than a smattering of partly learned words and phrases which is too often the result of such instruction.

The arrangement of the books into units with yearly and monthly objectives with specific instructions for each lesson reflects the authors' concern for the teacher. These specific instructions provide a detailed outline of the purposes and expected outcomes of each lesson. Thus they provide a blueprint for the teacher which, if followed, will allow him or her to become an effective instructor of English.

The fact that Hojel and Chávez have managed to incorporate all the elements which combine to make this series superior to other English-as-a-second-language programs is no accident. Both have backgrounds in regular and special education. Both have had graduate training in teacher education and learning theory.

Their commitment to applying the principles which educational and psychological research has shown are necessary for efficient learning can be attributed to their educational backgrounds, including advanced degrees earned by Dr. Chávez at the University of Kansas and by Hojel at Johns Hopkins University. However, the fact that they have made the activities and units so functional and interesting that children on whom the program was field tested looked forward to their English lessons with real anticipation can be attributed to their backgrounds as teachers. Hojel and Chávez are, in fact, the kind of teachers that have a genuine liking for and understanding of children such as those who will use these books. Such children will be fortunate indeed, for their chances of mastering English as a second language through this program will be excellent.

R. Vance Hall, Ph.D
Senior Scientist, Bureau of Child Research
Professor of Education and Department of Human Development
University of Kansas

This book belongs to:

name _____

grade _____

school _____

teacher _____

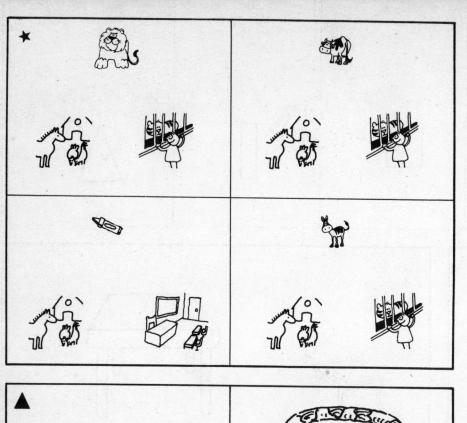

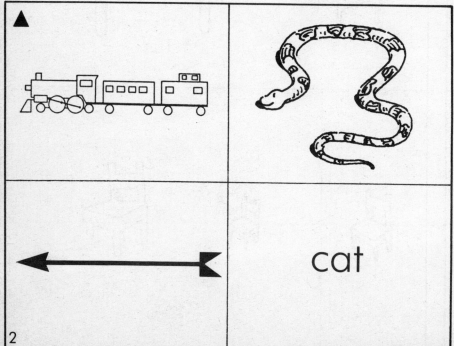

cat

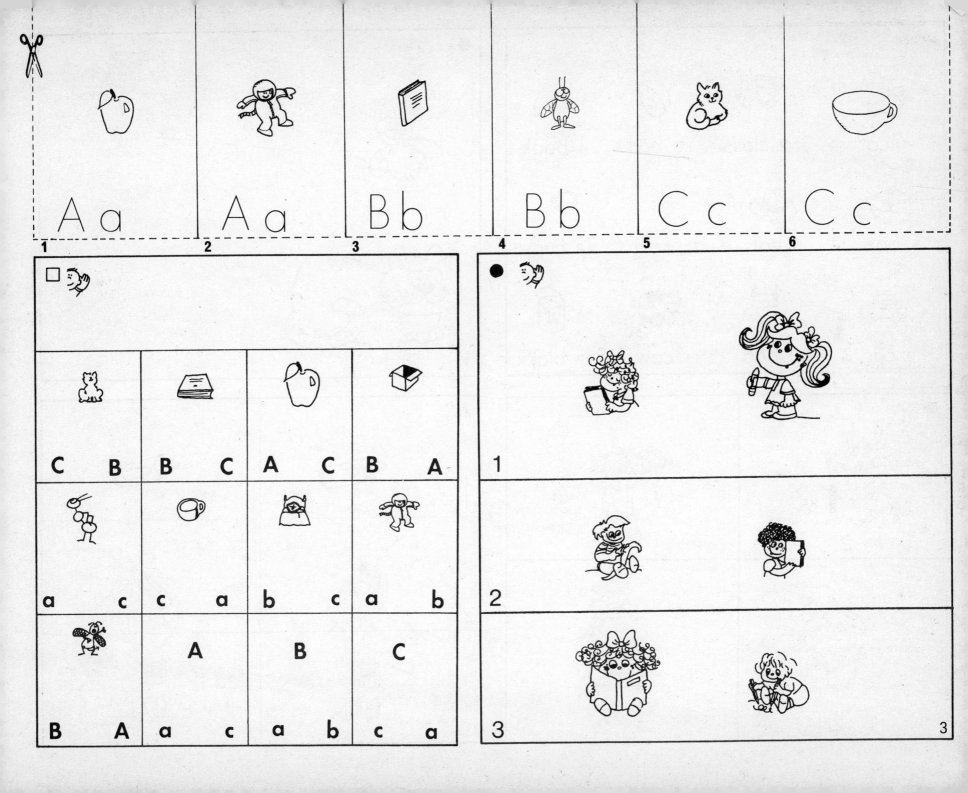

A a   A a   B b   B b   C c   C c

1   2   3   4   5   6

C B   B C   A C   B A

a c   c a   b c   a b

B A   A B   C

a c   a b   c a

1

2

3

3

1. cat
2. class
3. ball
4. book
5. box
6. hat
7. bug
8. cup
9. car
10. bed
11. cow
12. black

1 2

1 2

4   1 2

1 2

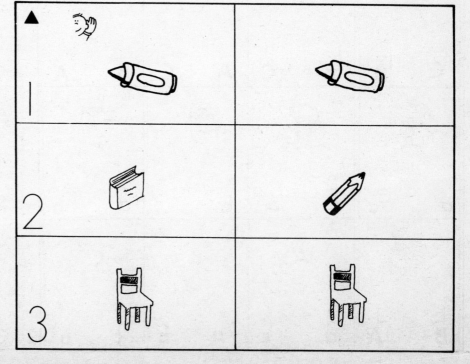

1

2

3

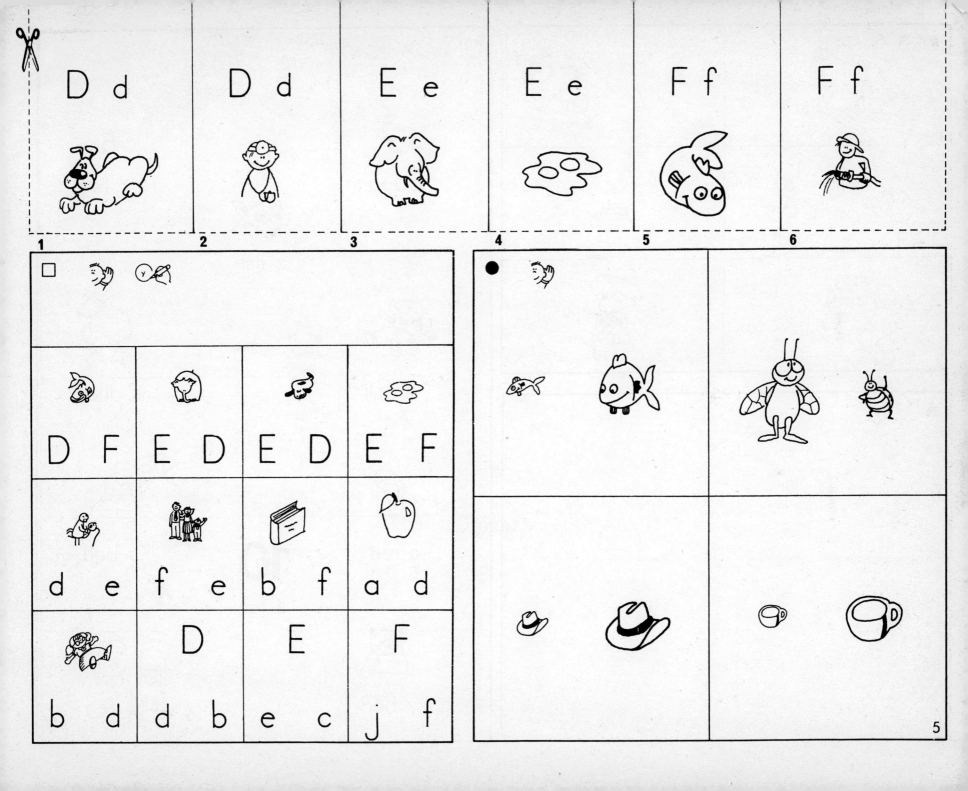

D d

D d

E e

E e

F f

F f

1 2 3 4 5 6

D F E D E D E F

d e f e b f a d

D E F

b d d b e c j f

5

6

★

1. dog

3. fish

5

4. five

2. doll

5. duck

6. red

10

8. ten

9. bed

7. bed

10. red

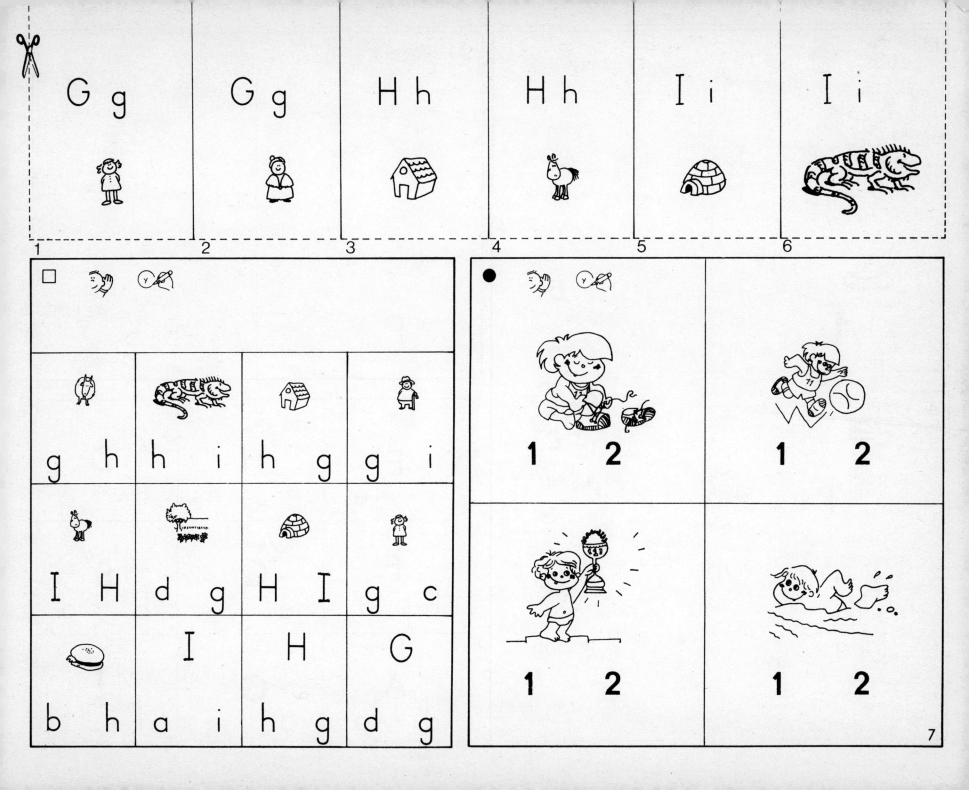

G g 　 G g 　 H h 　 H h 　 I i 　 I i

1　2　3　4　5　6

g　h　h　i　i　h　g　g　i

I　H　d　g　H　I　g　c

b　h　a　i　h　g　d　g

1　2　　1　2

1　2　　1　2

7

1. hen

3. fish

4. chick

2. hat

6

5. six

6. tiger

9. bug

8. pig

7. flag

10. dog

●

F f

B b

□

E	H	D
i e	f h	d g
1	2	3
F	C	B
h f	e c	b d
4	5	6
A	G	I
d a	d g	i l
7	8	9

★
1. black
2. fish
3. bed
4. cup
5. bug
10
6. ten

●
1. E F e B
2. c a A f
3. d c D C

1 2   1 2

☐
I
A
D
E
B
C
F

a
b
f
c
i
d
e

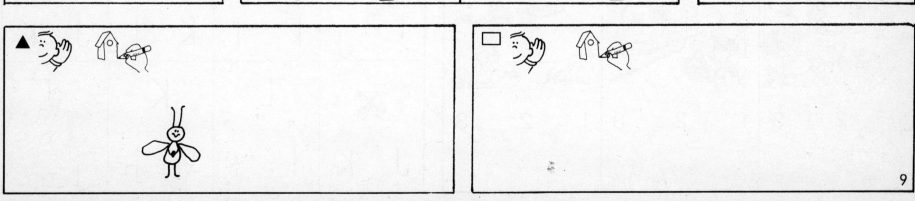

9

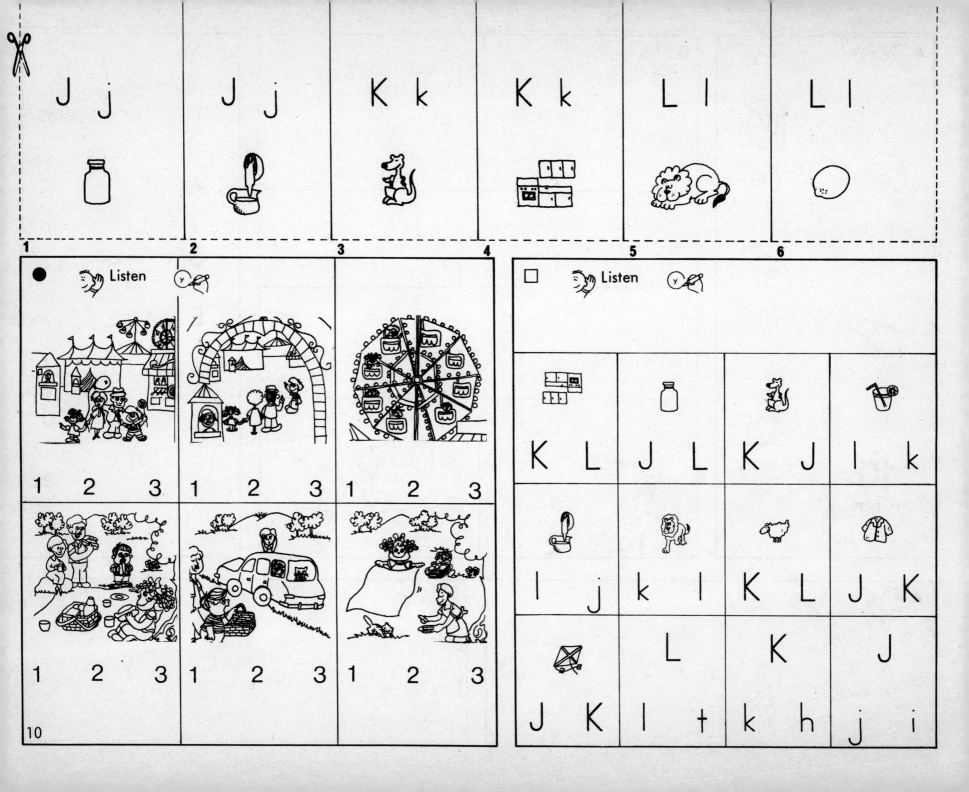

J j   J j   K k   K k   L l   L l

1   2   3   4   5   6

● 👂 Listen   ✏️

1   2   3
1   2   3
1   2   3
1   2   3
1   2   3
1   2   3

10

☐ 👂 Listen   ✏️

K L	J L	K J	l k
l j	k L	K L	J K
J K	L	K	J
J K	l t	k h	j i

▲

1. jar
2. jam
3. leg
4. lamp
5. pajamas
6. pink
7. book
8. seal

●

Listen

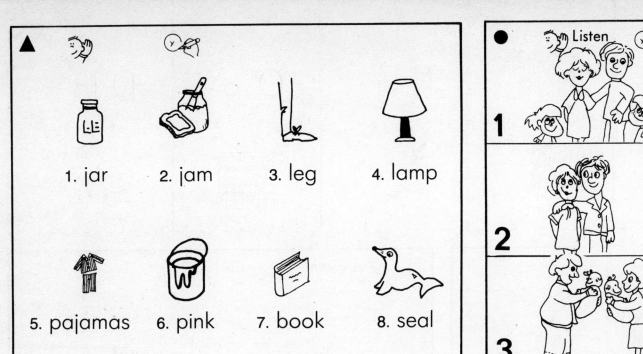

1

2

3

★

Listen

1. ball
2. doll
3. yellow
4. black
5. duck
6. chick

□

11

★ 👂 Listen ✏️ Circle

1. monkey 2. bottom 3. lemon 4. box

5. top 6. seven 7. green 8. ten

● 👂 Listen 🏠✏️

▲ 👂 Listen ✏️ Circle ✏️

1

2

3

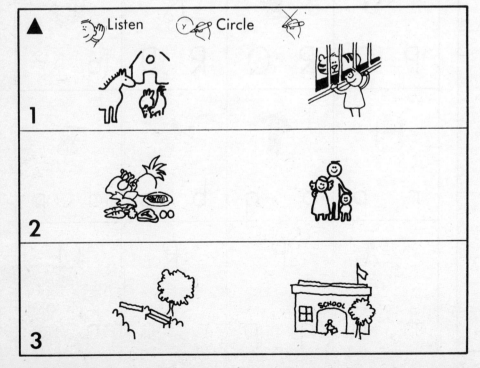

□ 👂 Listen 🏠✏️

M m   N n

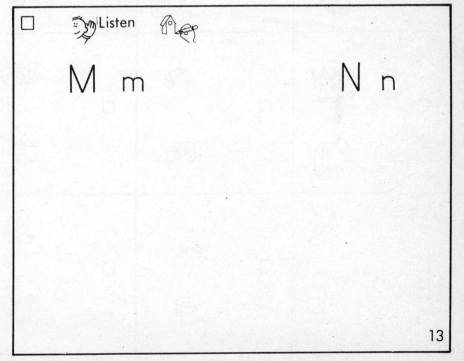

13

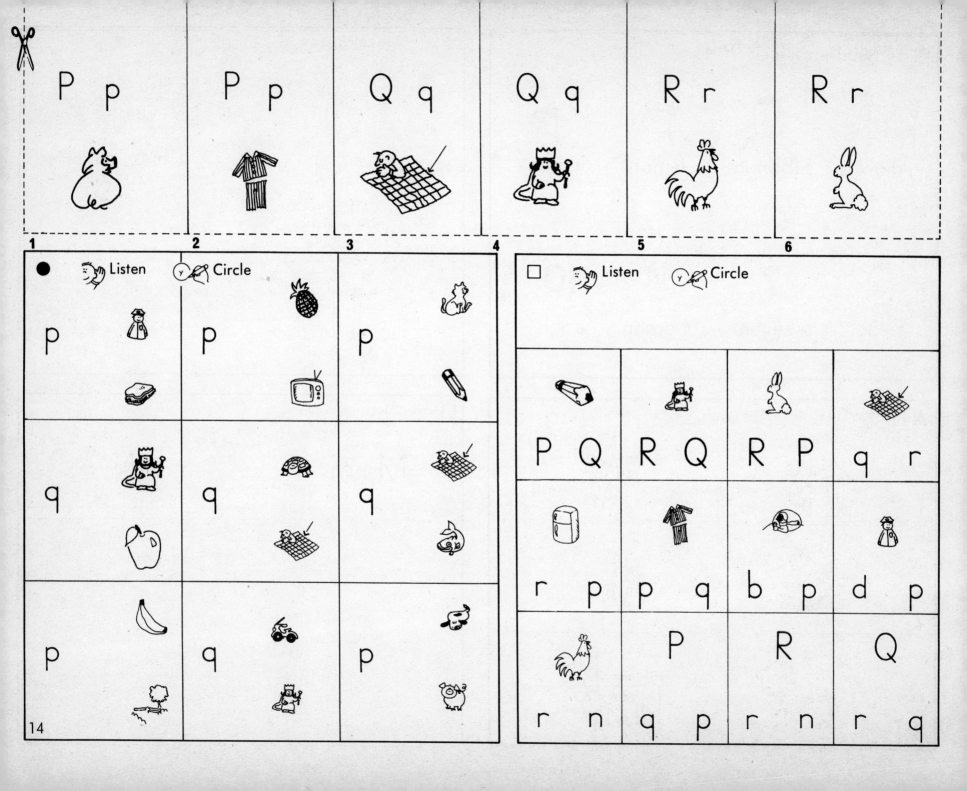

P p	P p	Q q	Q q	R r	R r

1   2   3   4   5   6

● 👂 Listen   ✐ Circle

□ 👂 Listen   ✐ Circle

14

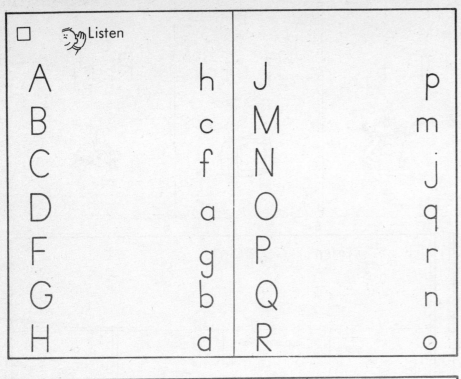

☐ 👂 Listen

A	h	J	p
B	c	M	m
C	f	N	j
D	a	O	q
F	g	P	r
G	b	Q	n
H	d	R	o

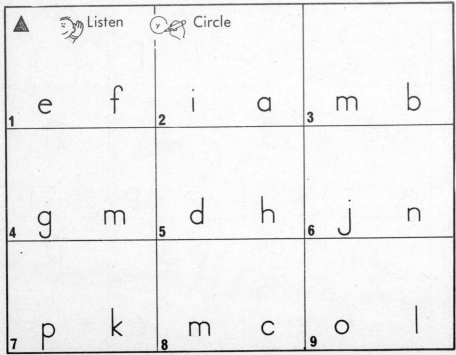

△ 👂 Listen   ✏ Circle

1. e f	2. i a	3. m b
4. g m	5. d h	6. j n
7. p k	8. m c	9. o l

★ 👂 Listen   ✏ Circle

1. top   2. cup

3. zipper   4. jar

5. car   6. four

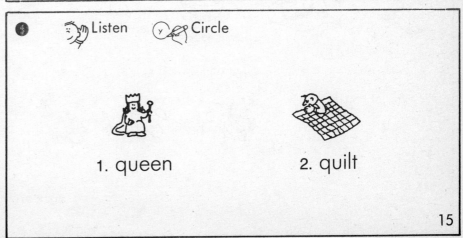

● 👂 Listen   ✏ Circle

1. queen   2. quilt

15

S s   S s   S s   T t   T t   T t

1   2   3   4   5   6

Listen

Listen   Circle

 s t	 t s	 t s	 t s
 s t	 s t	 s t	 s t
 p t	 s t	s c	t f

16

● 👂 Listen ✎ Circle

1	2	3
1	2	3
1	2	3

★ 👂 Listen

a	B	l
b	E	m
d	G	n
e	A	p
g	D	q
h	I	r
i	H	t

L
T
M
Q
R
N
P

□ 👂 Listen ✎ Circle

d t	t p	s t	**8**
s j	f s	s t	k s
t p	z s	ck 11	ck 11

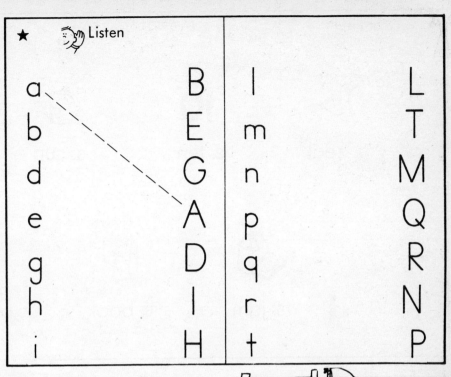 f t

▲ 👂 Listen

17

★ ✋ Listen ✏ Circle

1. seal **10** 3. cup 4. hat

5. jam 6. book 7. pajamas

□ ✋ Listen

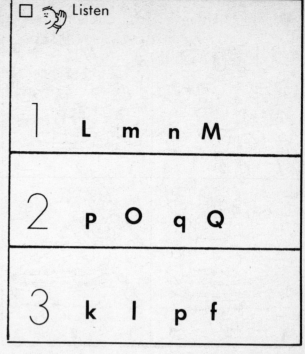

1 **L m n M**

2 **P O q Q**

3 **k l p f**

▲ ✋ Listen 🏠✏

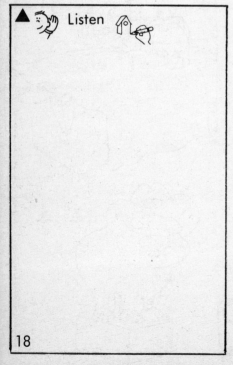

□ ✋ Listen

○ ✋ Listen

1

2

3

18

U u 	V v 	V v 	W w 	W w 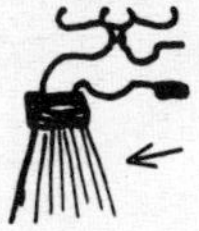	W w 

1   2   3   4   5   6

● Listen   Circle

 1 2 3	 1 2 3	 1 2 3
 1 2 3	 1 2 3	 1 2 3

☐ Listen   Circle

 U W	 U W	 W V	 W V
 M W	 B T	 P B	 d p
	U	W	V
v w	w u	v w	u v

19

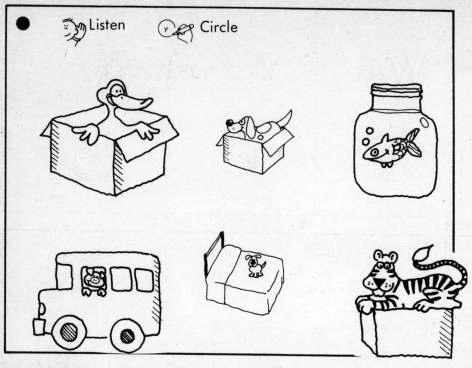

1. duck   2. cup   3. bug   4. bus

5. van   6. seven   7. wagon   8. water

7

20

X x

X x

6

Y y

Y y

Z z

Z z

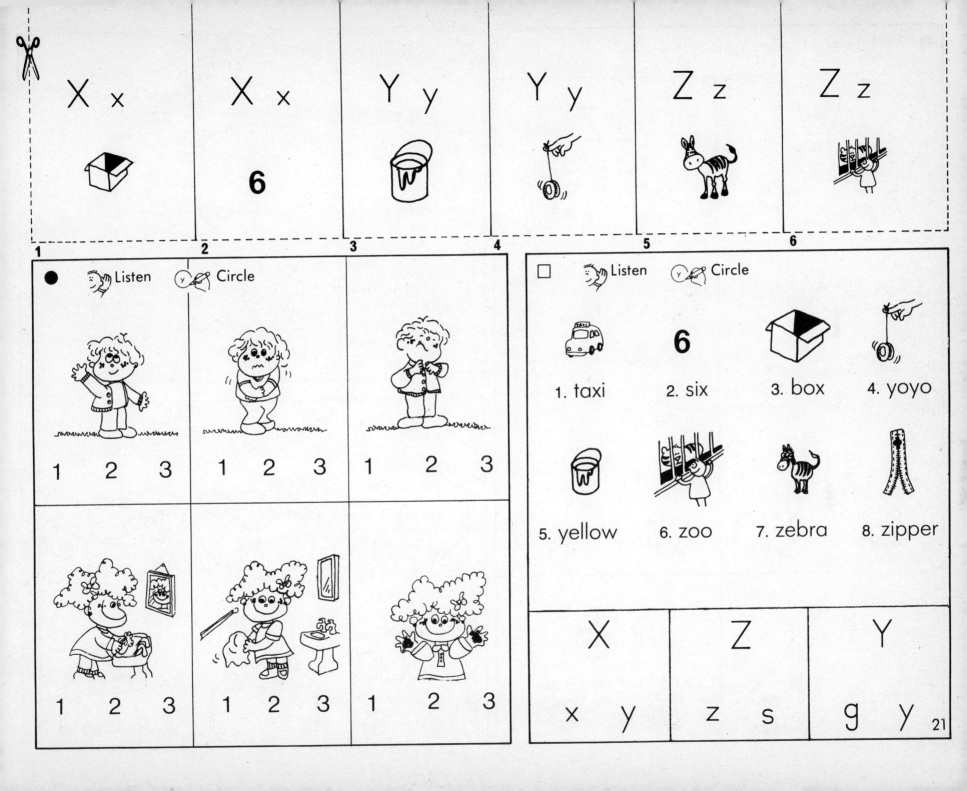

1 2 3 4 5 6

Listen   Circle

1 2 3   1 2 3   1 2 3

1 2 3   1 2 3   1 2 3

Listen   Circle

6

1. taxi   2. six   3. box   4. yoyo

5. yellow   6. zoo   7. zebra   8. zipper

X	Z	Y
x y	z s	g y

21

1. W

2. Z

3. X

4. Y

5. U

6. X   **6**

7. Z

8. W

22

1

2

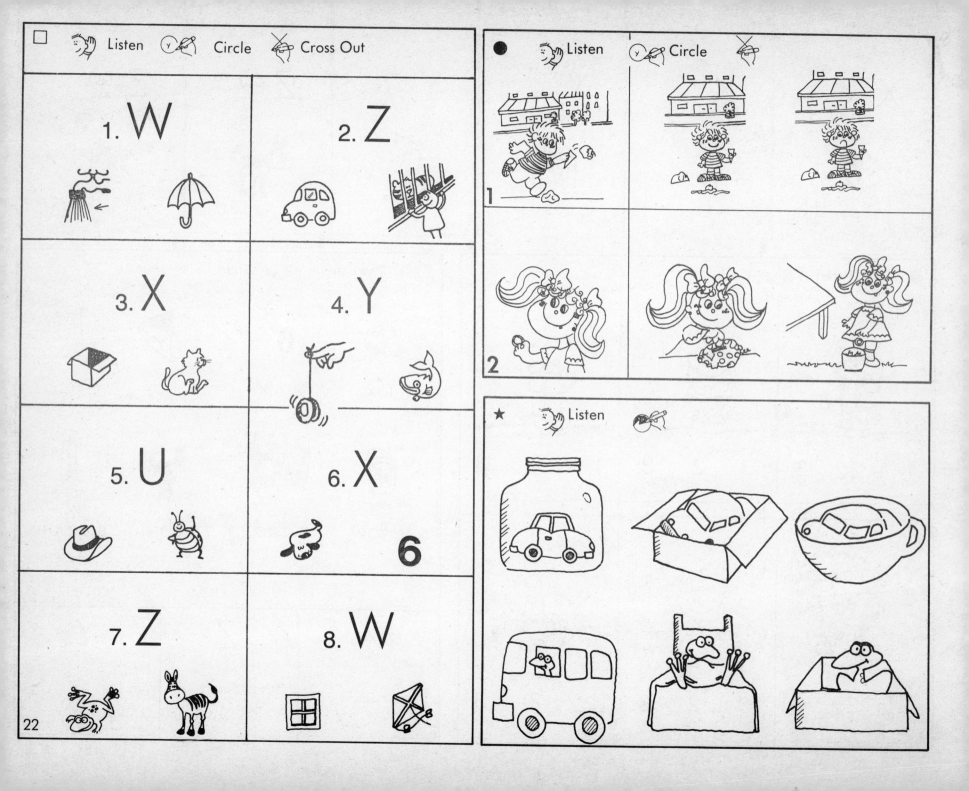

3

Th　th　Th　th　Sh　sh　Sh　sh　Sh　sh　Sh　sh

1　　2　　3　　4　　5　　6

● 👂 Listen 🔍 Circle

 1　2　3	 1　2　3	 1　2　3
 1　2　3	 1　2　3	 1　2　3

☐ 👂 Listen 🔍 Circle

		**3**	
th　b	sh　f	sh　th	th　sh

sh　z	th　sh	k　y	o　p
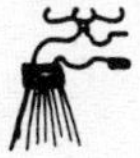			
m　w	q　r	th　sh	s　z

23

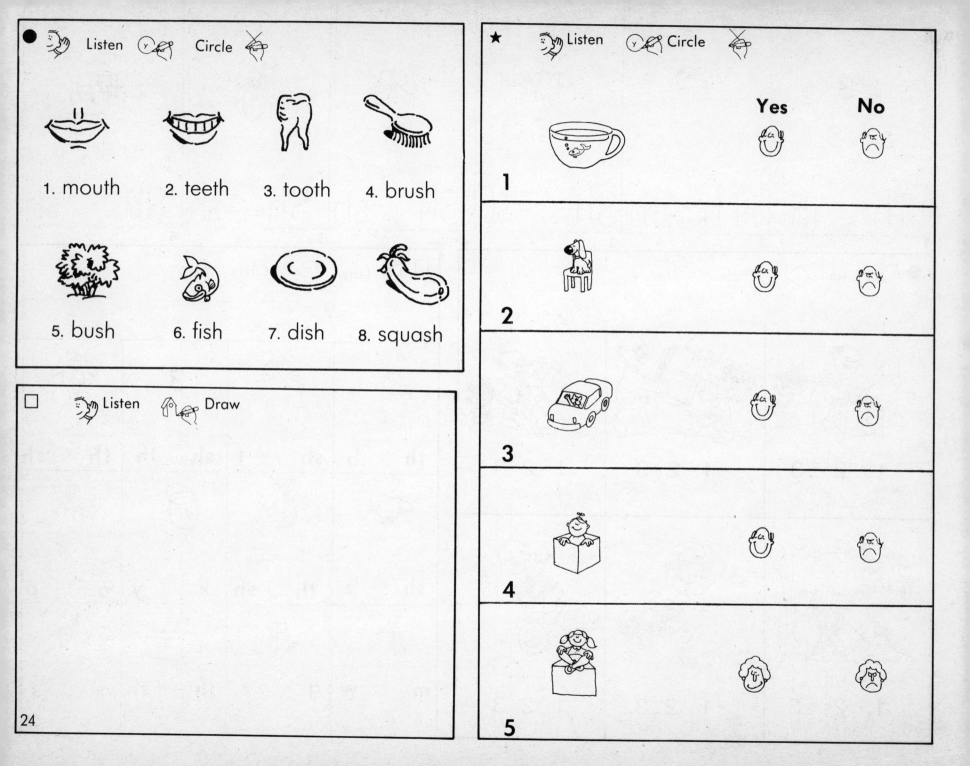

1. mouth   2. teeth   3. tooth   4. brush

5. bush   6. fish   7. dish   8. squash

□ 😊 Listen ✏️ Draw

★ 😊 Listen ✏️ Circle ✏️

Yes   **No**

1

2

3

4

5

24

Ch | ch | Ch | ch | Ch | ch | Wh | wh | Wh | wh | Wh | wh

1   2   3   4   5   6

□ Listen ✎ Circle

 ch b	 wh s	 ch th	 ch sh
 ch wh	 ch sh	 sh ch	th wh
			3
 sh ch	 sh ch	 sh wh	 ch wh

● Listen ✎ Circle

 1 2 3	 1 2 3	 1 2 3
 1 2 3	 1 2 3	 1 2 3

25

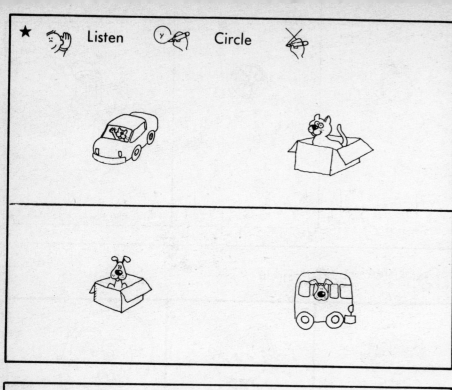 Listen   Circle

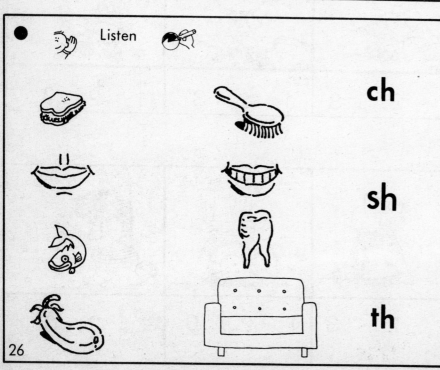

● Listen

ch

sh

th

26

■ Listen   Circle

1. chair

2. thumb

3. children

4. bathroom

5. shirt

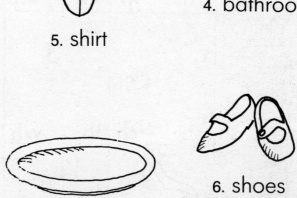

6. shoes

7. dish

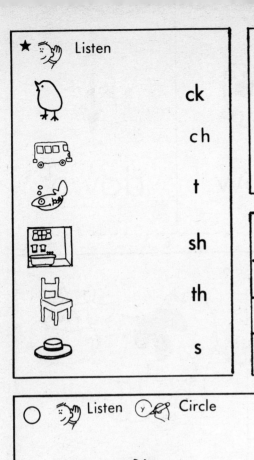

ck

ch

t

sh

th

s

● Listen

□ Listen Ⓨ Circle

1	Y	v	y	Z
2	S	t	c	s
3	Z	x	z	w

○ Listen Ⓨ Circle

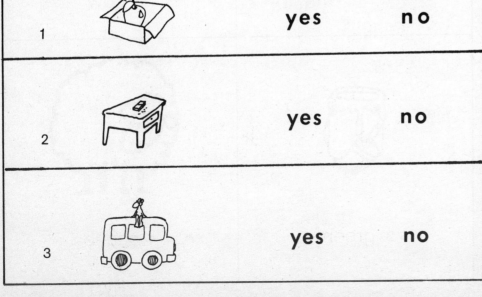

		yes	no
1		yes	no
2		yes	no
3		yes	no

▲ Listen

1

2

3

4

sheep | 3 three | green  | brown  | cow  | ↓ down

1 | 2 | 3 | 4 | 5 | 6

Listen

1. green
2. sheep 
3. tree 
4. cow 
5. brown 
6. down 
3
7. three
8. flower 

Listen   Color

1. brown
2. cow 
3. green 
4. sheep 

28

↓ down   🐄 cow   🌸 flower

3 three   🌳 tree   🐑 sheep

⬇   **3**   🐄

1. dish down   2. three thumb   3. cow cup

🌸   🐑   🌳

4. flower fish   5. shirt sheep   6. tree ten

1   sheep   🐑   🐱

2   flower   🌸   🐱

3   cow   🐱   🐄

4   three   🐴   **3**

5   tree   🌳   🐱

6   brown   🪣   🛏

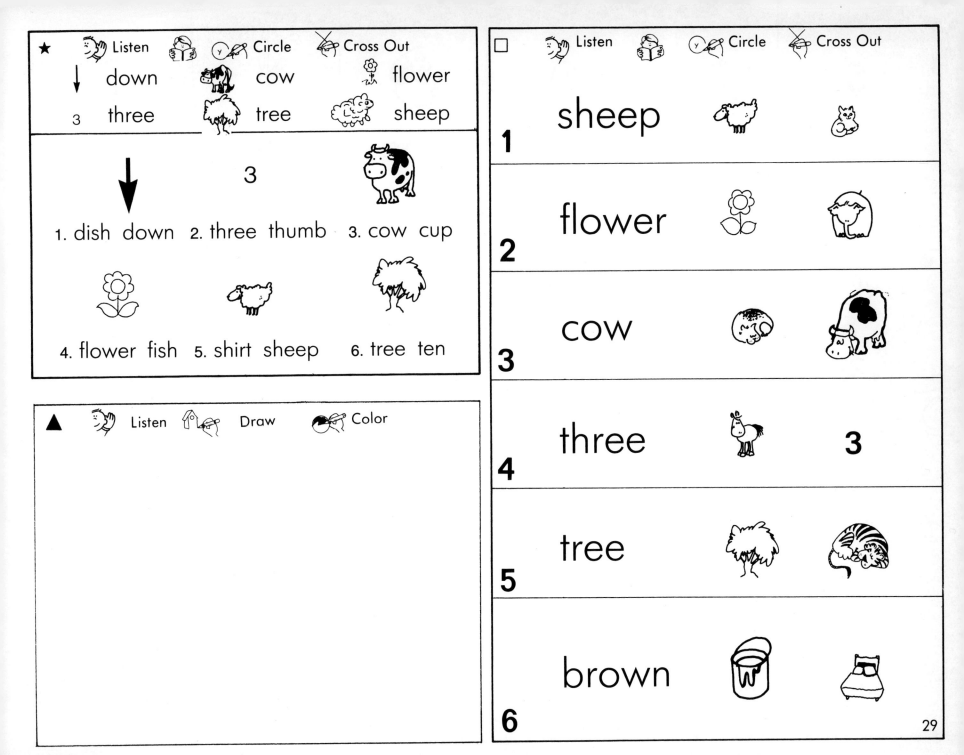

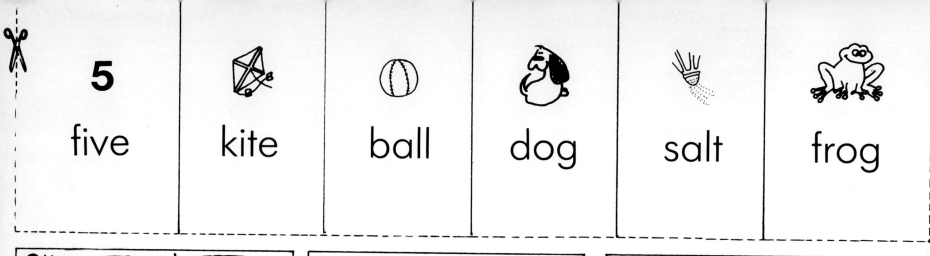

five   kite   ball   dog   salt   frog

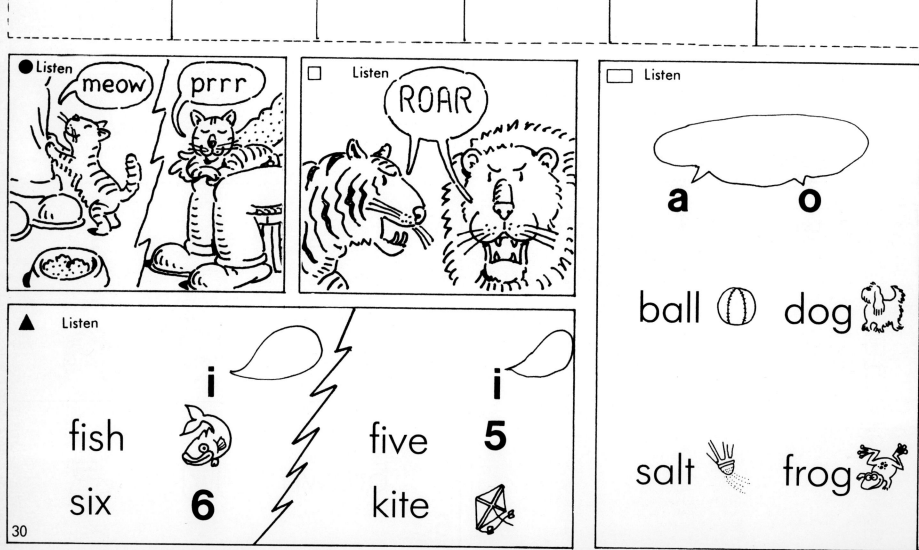

● Listen

meow   prrr

□ Listen

ROAR

□ Listen

a   o

ball   dog

salt   frog

▲ Listen

i   i

fish   five   5

six   6   kite

30

ball   salt   **5** five

dog   frog   kite

5

1. ball boy   2. fish five   3. cat kite

4. frog book   5. dog salt   6. dish dog

5

10

6

K

down   kite   frog   sheep   dog   cow

31

COW

three

green

sheep

fish   kite

white

5   **6**

five   six

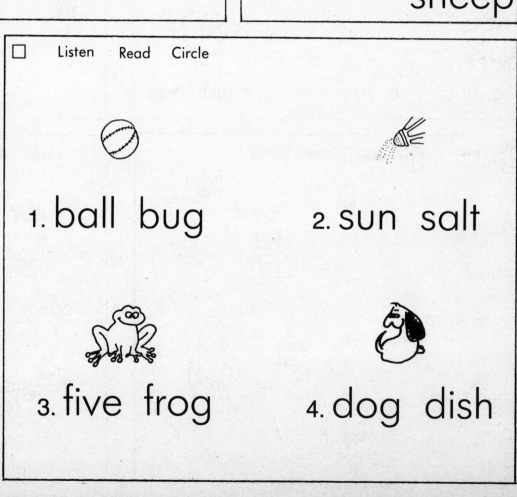

1. ball bug   2. sun salt

3. five frog   4. dog dish

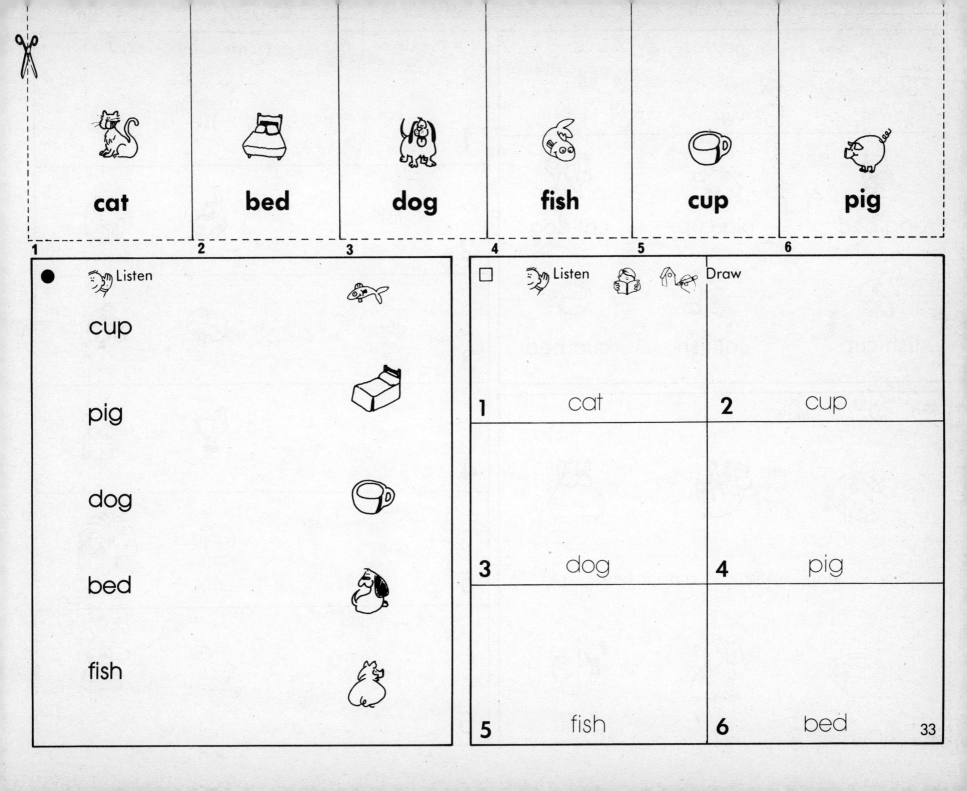					
cat	**bed**	**dog**	**fish**	**cup**	**pig**
1	2	3	4	5	6

● 👂 Listen

cup

pig

dog

bed

fish

☐ 👂 Listen   👦📖 🏠✏ Draw

1	cat	2	cup
3	dog	4	pig
5	fish	6	bed

33

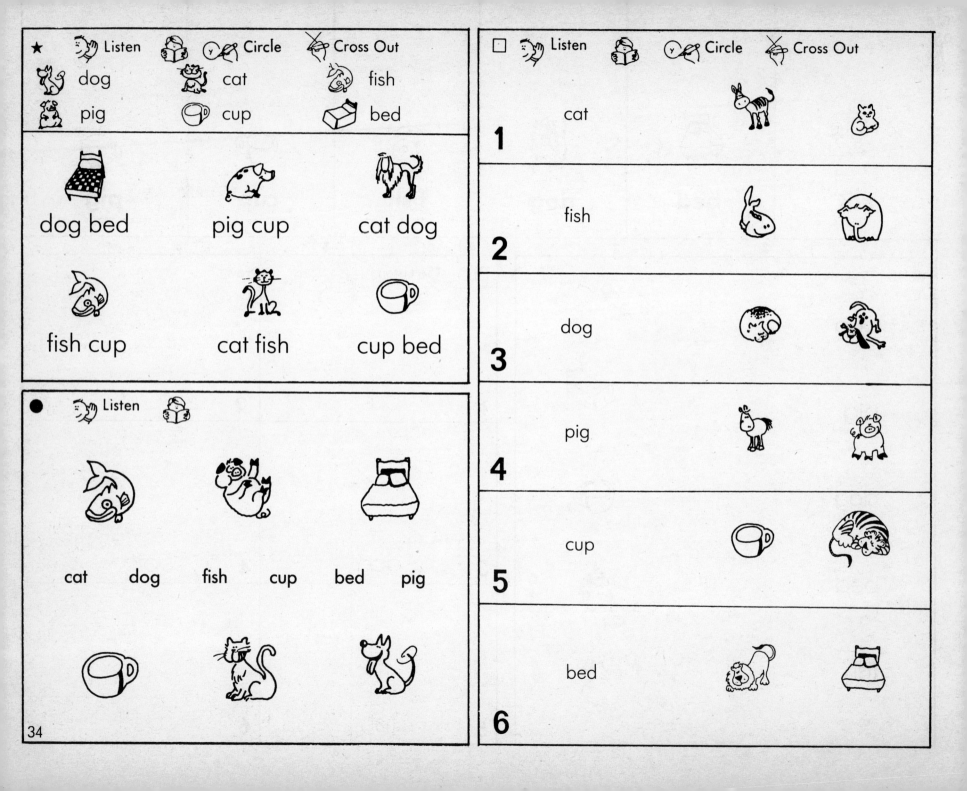
dog   cat   fish

pig   cup   bed

dog bed   pig cup   cat dog

fish cup   cat fish   cup bed

●   Listen

cat   dog   fish   cup   bed   pig

34

□   Listen   Circle   Cross Out

1   cat

2   fish

3   dog

4   pig

5   cup

6   bed

It	is	a	It	is	a

1   2   3   4   5   6

☐ Listen. 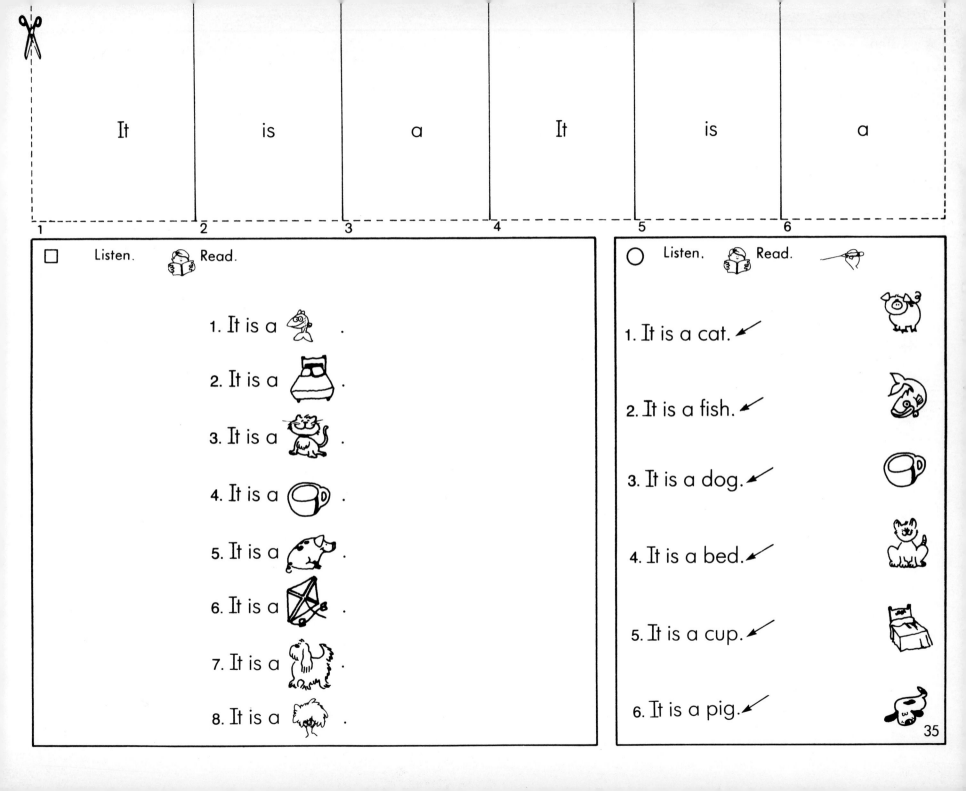 Read.

1. It is a   .

2. It is a   .

3. It is a   .

4. It is a   .

5. It is a   .

6. It is a   .

7. It is a   .

8. It is a   .

○ Listen. Read.

1. It is a cat.

2. It is a fish.

3. It is a dog.

4. It is a bed.

5. It is a cup.

6. It is a pig.

35

★ Listen. Circle.

1 It is a ____ .

2 It is a ____ .

3 It is a ____ .

4 It is a ____ .

5 It is a ____ .

6 It is a ____ .

7 It is a ____ .

8 It is a ____ .

36

■ Listen. Read.

1 It is a ____ .   fish

2 It is a ____ .   dog

3 It is a ____ .   pig

4 It is a ____ .   bed.

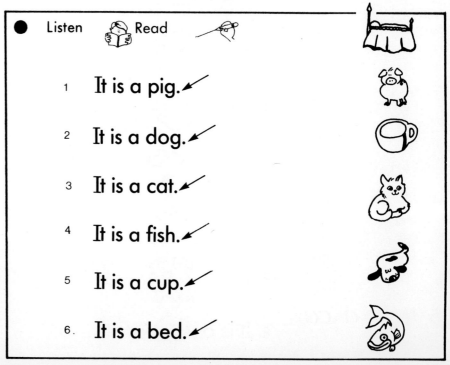

● Listen. Read.

1 It is a pig.

2 It is a dog.

3 It is a cat.

4 It is a fish.

5 It is a cup.

6. It is a bed.

bug	**car**	**pink**	**hat**	**red**	**green**
1	2	3	4	5	6

★ Listen. Read.

1 *It is a cup.*

2 *It is a hat.*

3 *It is a bug.*

4 *It is a fish.*

5 *It is a car.*

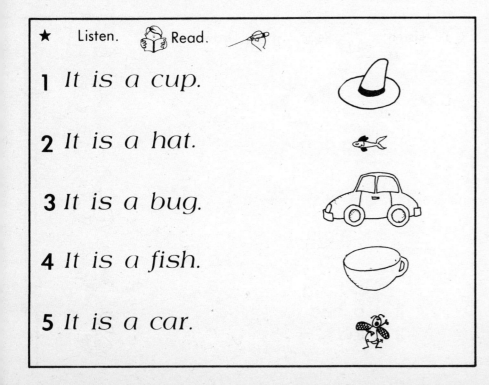

● Listen. Read. Circle. Cross Out.

green red   red pink   pink green

1

green   pink   red

2

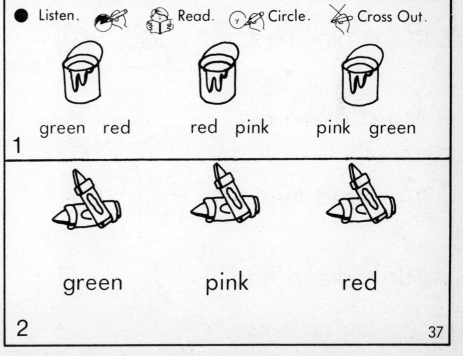

37

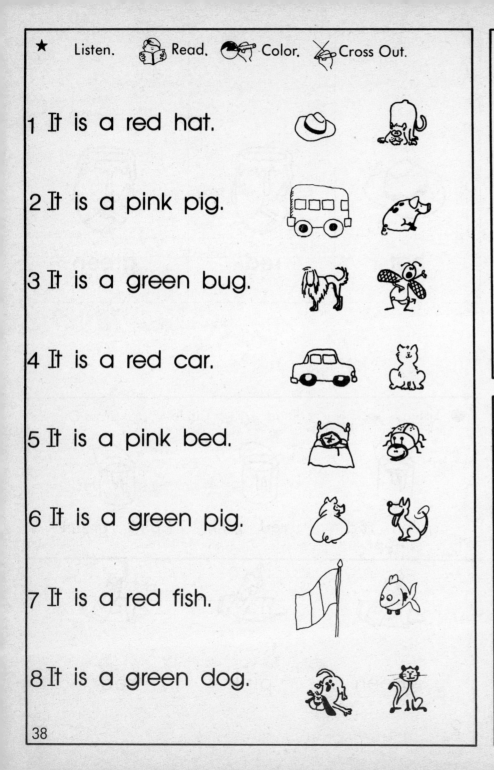

1 It is a red hat.

2 It is a pink pig.

3 It is a green bug.

4 It is a red car.

5 It is a pink bed.

6 It is a green pig.

7 It is a red fish.

8 It is a green dog.

38

red   bed   cat   hat   pink   pig

bug   dog   car   cup   bug   pig

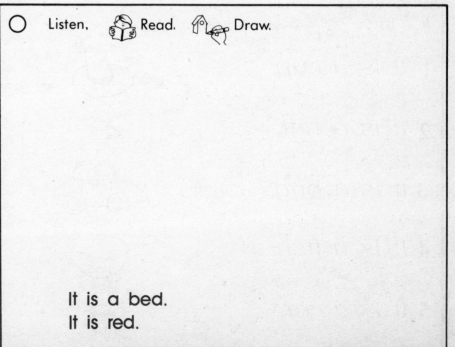

It is a bed.
It is red.

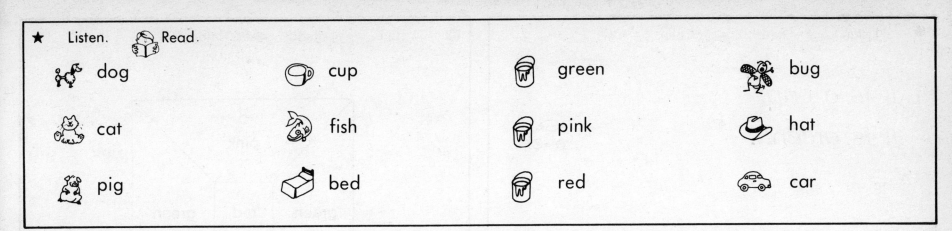

dog   cup   green   bug

cat   fish   pink   hat

pig   bed   red   car

● Listen. Read.

1 It is a cup.

2 It is a dog.

3 It is a fish.

4 It is a cat.

5 It is a pig.

☐ Listen. Read. Color.

1 It is green.

2 It is red.

3 It is red.

4 It is pink.

5 It is green.

39

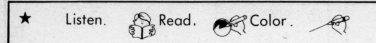

1 *It is a cup.*

It is green.

2 It is a car.

It is red.

3 It is a pig.

It is pink.

4 It is a hat.

It is pink.

40

● Listen. Read. Color.

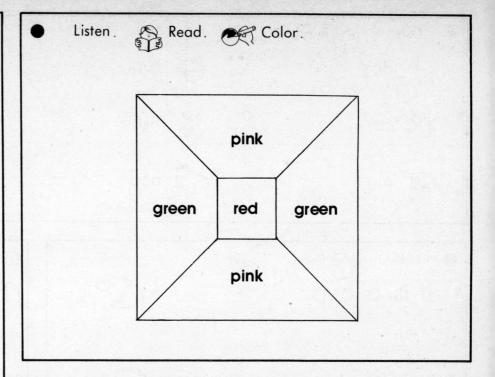

■ Listen. Read. Color.

It is a red pig.

It is a green fish.

It is a red bug.

It is a pink bed.

It is a green hat.

It is a pink car.

★ Listen. Read. Circle.

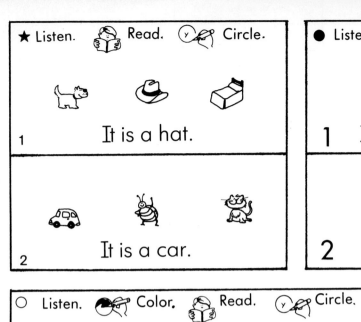

1   It is a hat.

2   It is a car.

● Listen. Color.

1   It is a pink hat.

2   It is a green cup.

○ Listen. Color. Read. Circle.

1   It is a car.
     It is pink.

2   It is a bug.
     It is green.

☐ Listen.

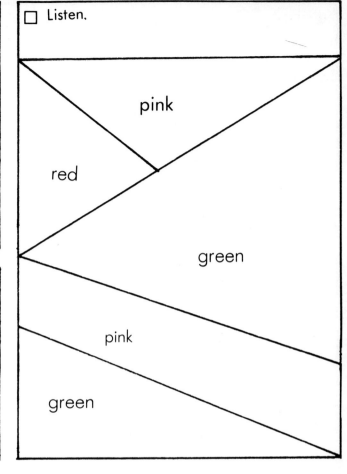

pink

red

green

pink

green

▲ Listen.

1   hat
     cat

2   bug
     dog

3   red
     bed

4   cat
     car

☐ Listen. Read. Draw.

It is a green bug.

41

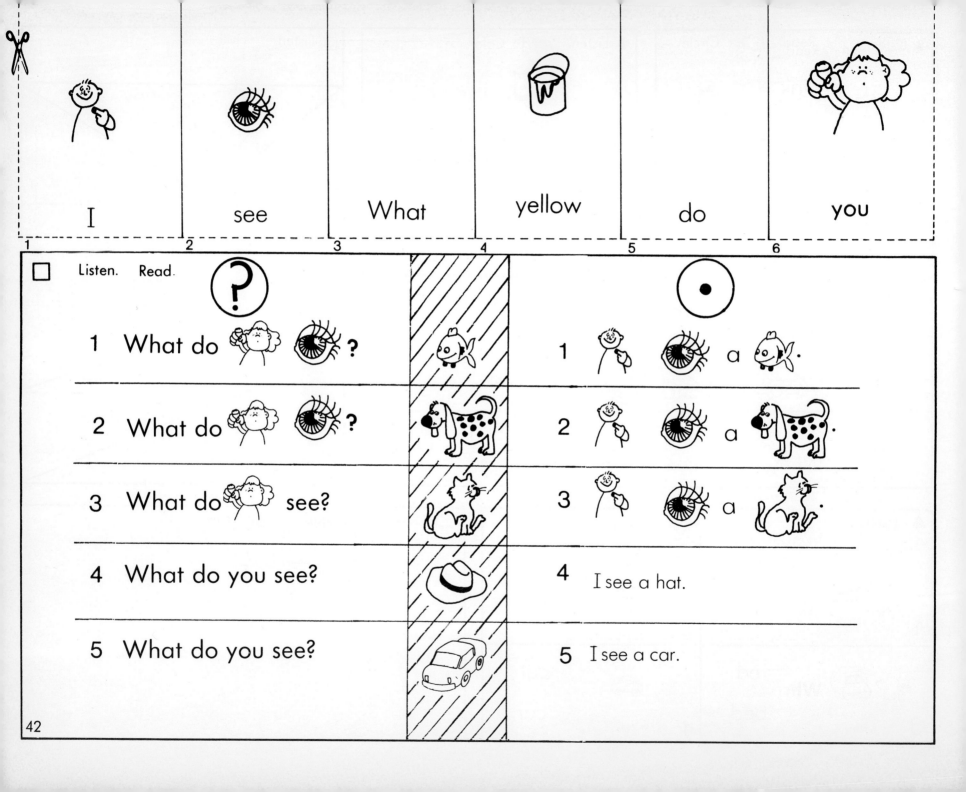

I

see

What

yellow

do

you

1 2 3 4 5 6

Listen. Read.

1 What do ? ?

2 What do ? ?

3 What do see?

4 What do you see?

5 What do you see?

1 a .

2 a .

3 a .

4 I see a hat.

5 I see a car.

42

Listen. Read. Color.

I see a pink fish.

I see a yellow pig.

I see a yellow hat.

I see a yellow bug.

I see a yellow car.

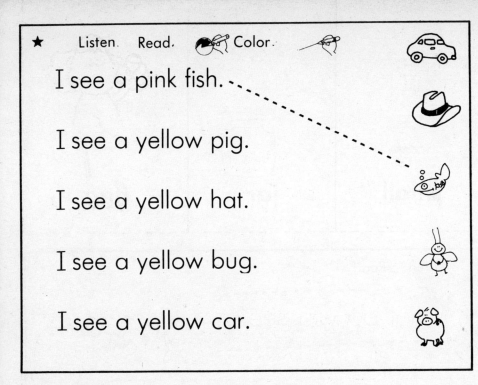

☐ Listen. Read. Draw.

I see a yellow cup.

○ Listen. Read. Draw.

1 **What do you see?**

2 **What do you see?**

3 **What do you see?**

4 **What do you see?**

1 I see a green cup.

2 I see a yellow hat.

3 I see a red bug.

4 I see a pink bed.

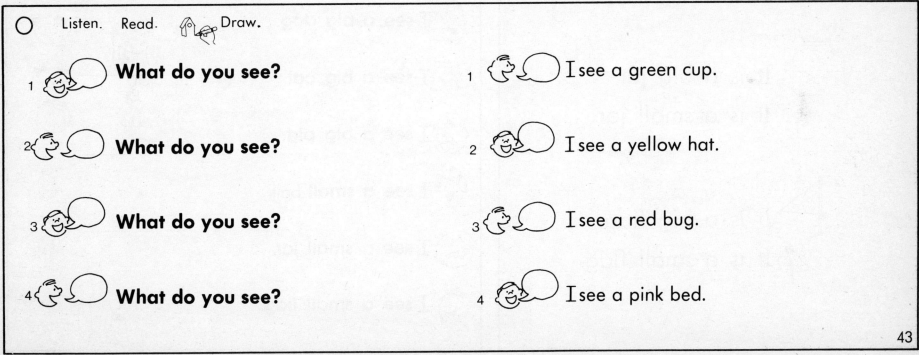

43

big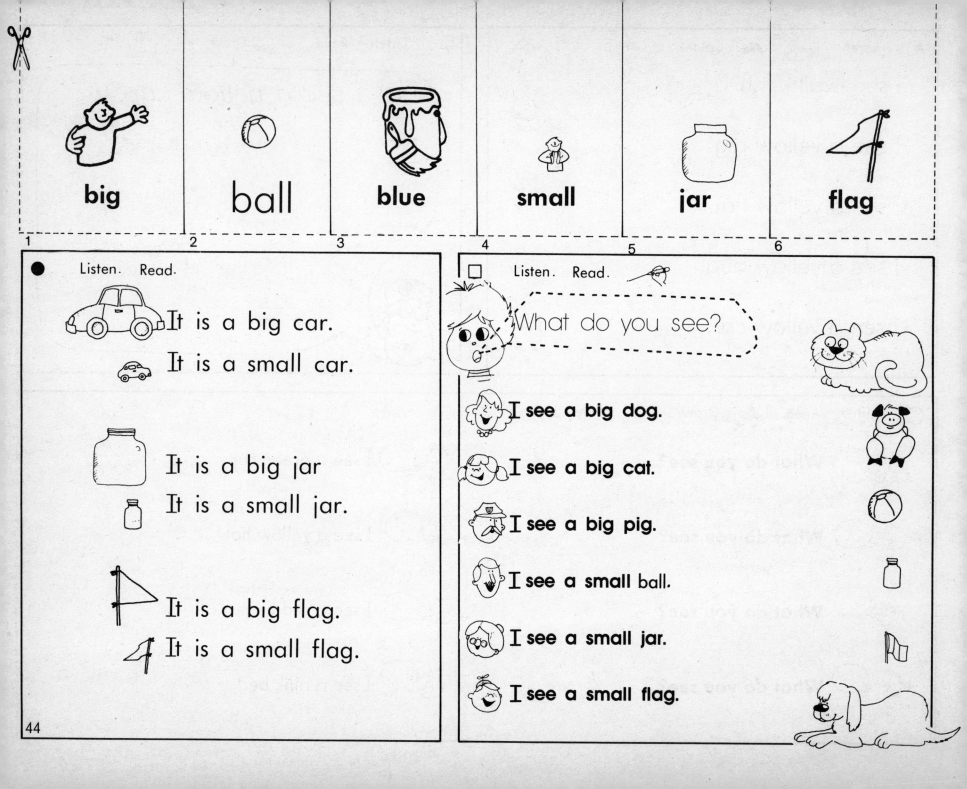

ball

blue

small

jar

flag

1   2   3   4   5   6

Listen. Read.

It is a big car.

It is a small car.

It is a big jar

It is a small jar.

It is a big flag.

It is a small flag.

44

Listen. Read.

What do you see?

I see a big dog.

I see a big cat.

I see a big pig.

I see a small ball.

I see a small jar.

I see a small flag.

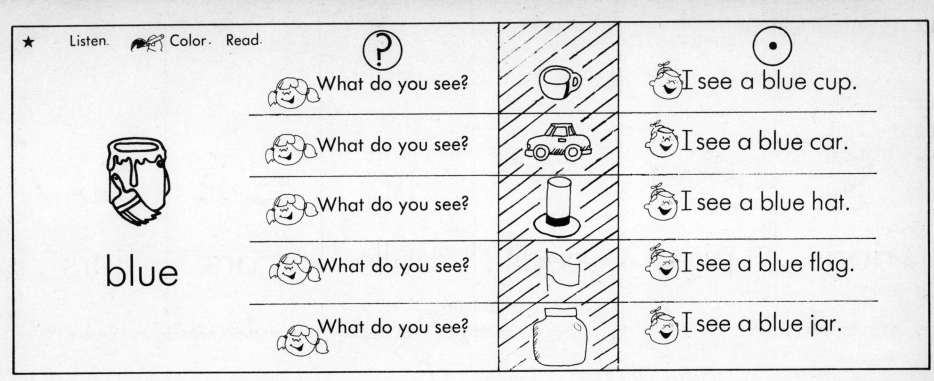

★ Listen. Color. Read.

? What do you see? — I see a blue cup.

What do you see? — I see a blue car.

What do you see? — I see a blue hat.

What do you see? — I see a blue flag.

What do you see? — I see a blue jar.

blue

☐ Listen. Read. Circle. Cross Out.

I see a big yellow hat.

I see a small blue car.

● Listen. Read.

jar   flag   car   big   small

45

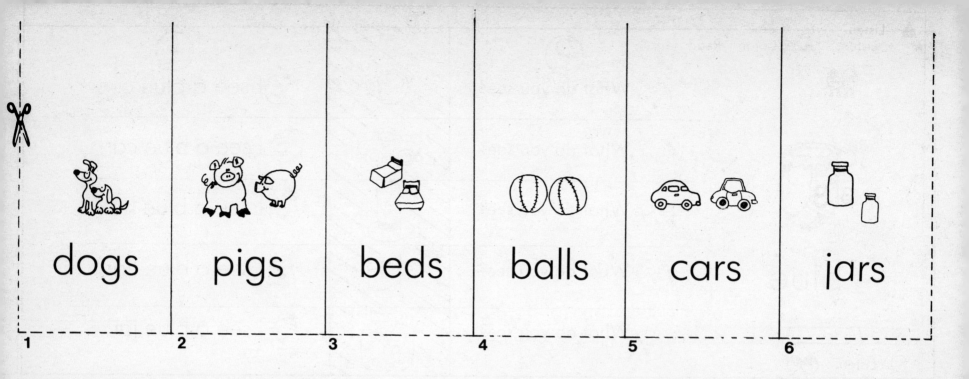

1	2	3	4	5	6
dogs	pigs	beds	balls	cars	jars

● Listen.   Read.

dog	dogs
pig	pigs
flag	flags
car	cars
jar	jars

46

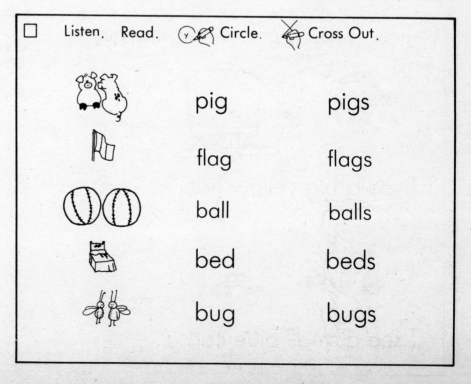

□ Listen. Read.   Circle.   Cross Out.

pig	pigs
flag	flags
ball	balls
bed	beds
bug	bugs

▲ Listen. Color.

cow   cows

tree   trees

three   threes

five   fives

shoe   shoes

☐ Listen. Draw.

○ Listen.

47

1	2	3	4	5	6
hats	cats	cups	shirts	chick	chicks

★ Listen.   Read.

cat		cats
hat		hats
shirt		shirts
cup		cups
chick		chicks

48

☐ Listen.   Circle.   Cross Out.

	cup	cups
	shirt	shirts
	hat	hats
	chick	chicks
	cat	cats

★ Listen . Read . Circle . Color .

It is a chick

It is small.

It is yellow.

□ Listen . Read . Draw.

I see six black hats.

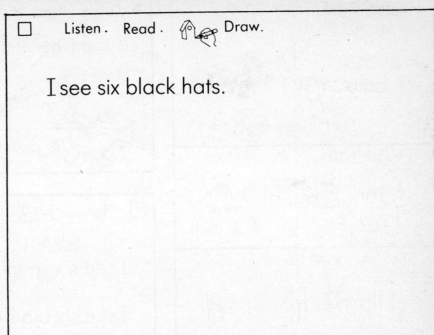

● Listen . Read .

I see five small shirts.

I see five small chicks.

I see five big shirts.

▲ Listen . Read . Circle .

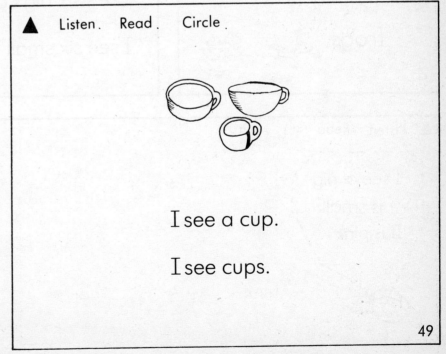

I see a cup.

I see cups.

49

★ Listen. Read. Circle.

1 balls

2 jar

3 flags

4 frogs

● Listen. Read. Circle.

It is a frog.
It is big.

☐ Listen. 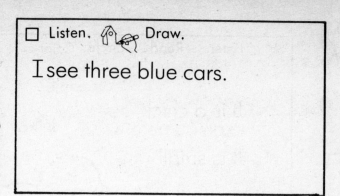 Draw.

I see three blue cars.

○ Listen. Read.

I see six small cats.

I see six big bugs.

I see six big cats.

I see six small bugs.

▲ Listen. Read. 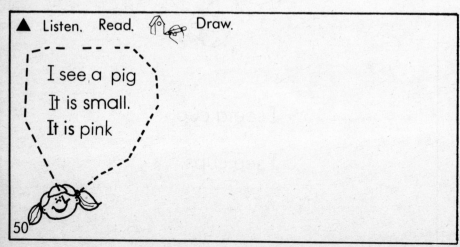 Draw.

I see a pig
It is small.
It is pink

50

☐ Listen. Read. Circle.

I see ducks.

I see a duck.

10	6	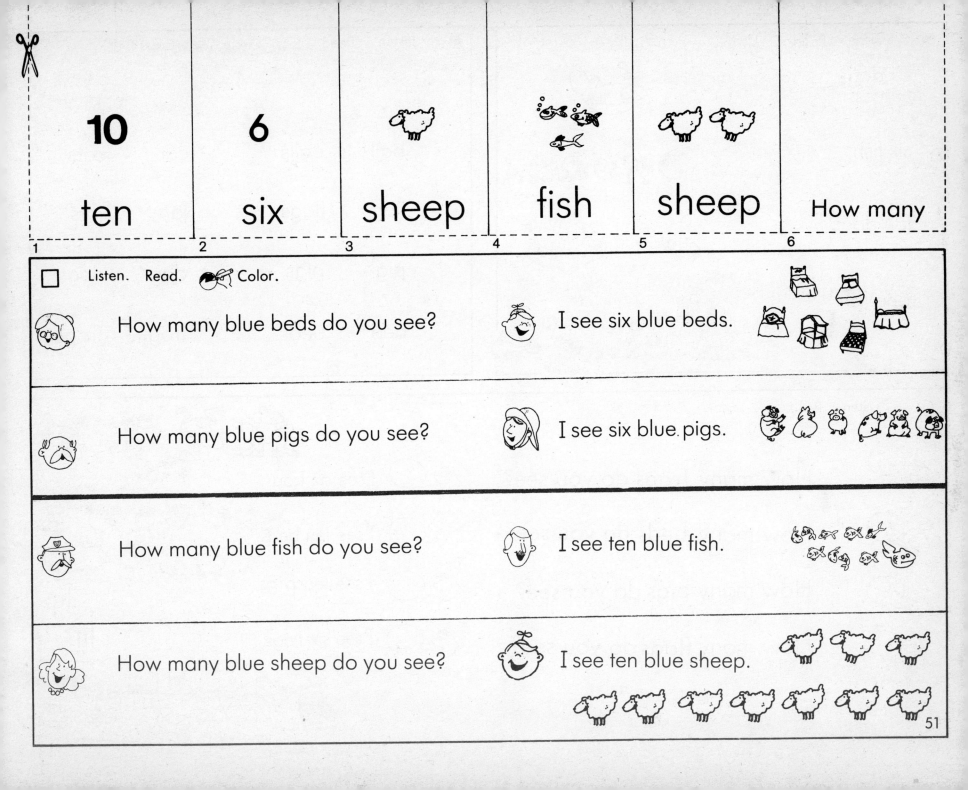			
ten	six	sheep	fish	sheep	How many
1	2	3	4	5	6

☐ Listen. Read. Color.

How many blue beds do you see?   I see six blue beds.

How many blue pigs do you see?   I see six blue pigs.

How many blue fish do you see?   I see ten blue fish.

How many blue sheep do you see?   I see ten blue sheep.

51

★ Listen. Read.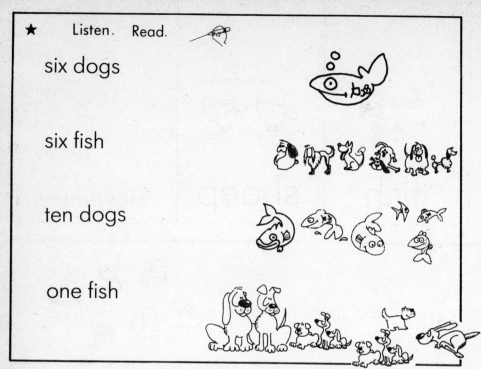

six dogs

six fish

ten dogs

one fish

● Listen. Read. Circle. Cross Out.

ball	balls	car	cars
flag	flags	jar	jars
pig	pigs	dog	dogs
bed	beds	frog	frogs

○ Listen. Read.

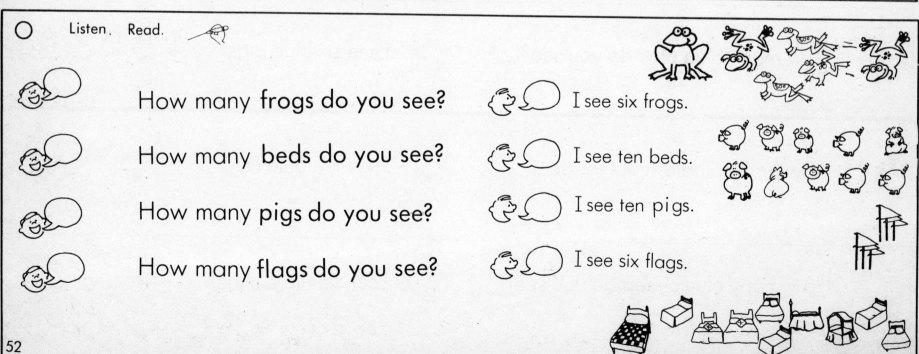

How many **frogs** do you see?   I see six frogs.

How many **beds** do you see?   I see ten beds.

How many **pigs** do you see?   I see ten pigs.

How many **flags** do you see?   I see six flags.

52

3	7	4	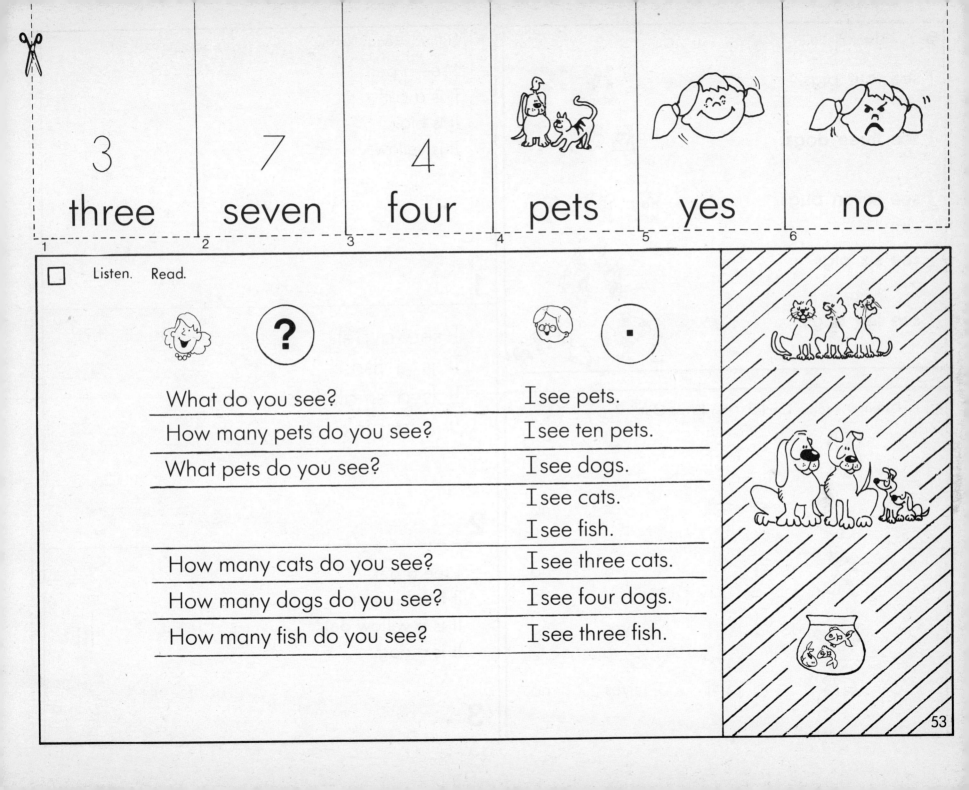		
three	seven	four	pets	yes	no

1   2   3   4   5   6

☐   Listen.   Read.

What do you see?	I see pets.
How many pets do you see?	I see ten pets.
What pets do you see?	I see dogs.
	I see cats.
	I see fish.
How many cats do you see?	I see three cats.
How many dogs do you see?	I see four dogs.
How many fish do you see?	I see three fish.

53

I see four pigs.

I see three dogs.

I see seven bugs.

I see six pigs.

I see ten bugs.

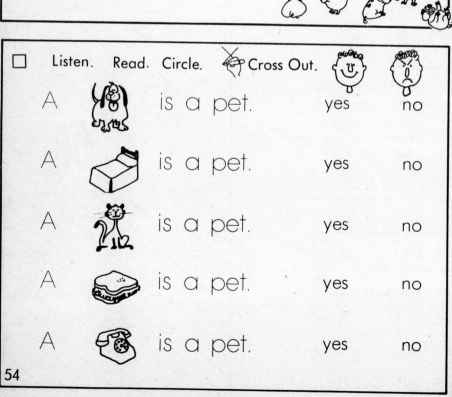

□ Listen. Read. Circle. Cross Out.

A   is a pet.   yes   no

A   is a pet.   yes   no

A   is a pet.   yes   no

A   is a pet.   yes   no

A   is a pet.   yes   no

54

★ Listen. Read. Draw.

I see a pet.
It is a cat.
It is big.
It is yellow.

1

I see a pet.
It is a fish.
It is a small fish.
It is a pink fish.

2

I see a pet.
It is a big pet.
It is a yellow pet.
It is a dog.

3

duck

5

five

and

black

ducks

have

| 1 | 2 | 3 | 4 | 5 | 6 |

Listen. Read.

What pets do you have?

I have five black dogs.

I have five black fish.

I have five black ducks.

I have five black bugs.

I have five black cats.

WOW!

Listen. Read.

I have a dog and a cat.

I have a jar and three bugs.

I have four fish and a dog.

I have five dogs and a cat.

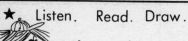

★ Listen. Read. Draw.

What do you see?

I see a big duck.
It is black and yellow.

1

How many bugs do you see?

I see three green bugs and four blue bugs.

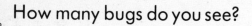

2

What do you have?

I have a small flag.
It is yellow and black.

3

● Listen. Read. Circle. ✃ Cross Out.

I have a jar and a bug.

I have a hat and a flag.

I have a dog and a duck.

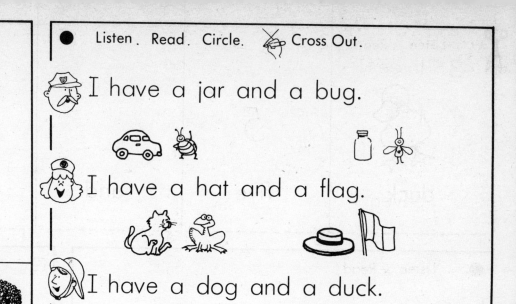

▲ Listen. Read. 🖍 Color.

five = black   **six = blue**   **ten = red**

three = yellow   **four = green**   **seven = pink**

★ Listen. Read.

3 three

4 four

5 five

7 seven

you

how many

big

small

car

jar

flag

frog

blue

black

what

do

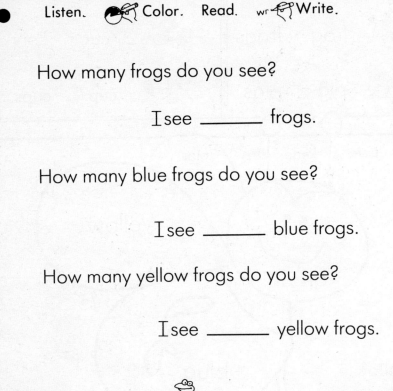

● Listen. Color. Read. Write.

How many frogs do you see?

I see _____ frogs.

How many blue frogs do you see?

I see _____ blue frogs.

How many yellow frogs do you see?

I see _____ yellow frogs.

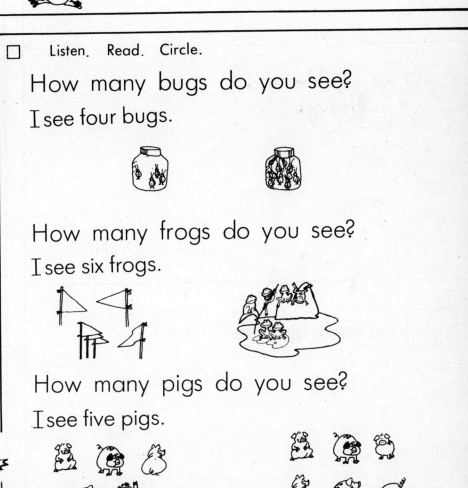

☐ Listen. Read. Circle.

How many bugs do you see?
I see four bugs.

How many frogs do you see?
I see six frogs.

How many pigs do you see?
I see five pigs.

57

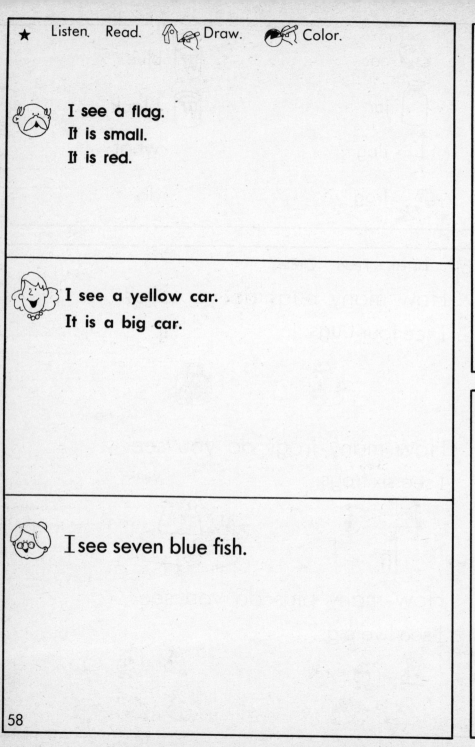

I see a flag.
It is small.
It is red.

I see a yellow car.
It is a big car.

I see seven blue fish.

○ Listen. Read. Circle. ✗ Cross Out.

dog	dogs		flag	flags
bug	bugs		jar	jars
duck	ducks		hat	hats
frog	frogs		car	cars
pig	pigs		cup	cups

● Listen. Read. Color.

yellow

green

yellow

blue

green

★ Listen. Read. 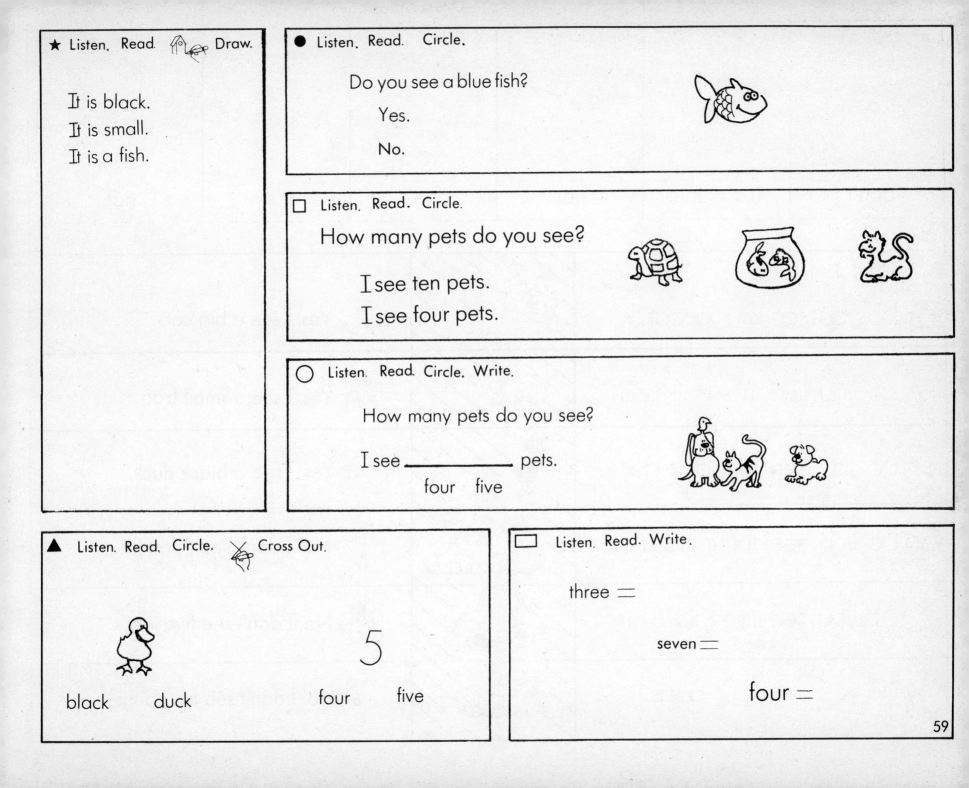 Draw.

It is black.
It is small.
It is a fish.

● Listen. Read. Circle.

Do you see a blue fish?

   Yes.

   No.

□ Listen. Read. Circle.

How many pets do you see?

  I see ten pets.

  I see four pets.

○ Listen. Read. Circle. Write.

How many pets do you see?

I see _____ pets.
      four five

▲ Listen. Read. Circle. Cross Out.

black   duck

5

four   five

□ Listen. Read. Write.

three =

seven =

four =

59

● Listen.   Read.

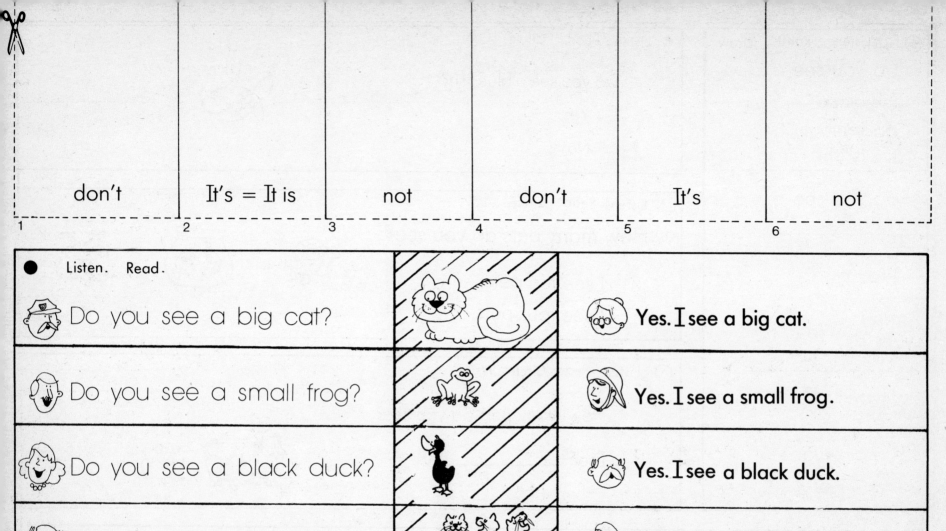

Do you see a big cat? | Yes. I see a big cat.

Do you see a small frog? | Yes. I see a small frog.

Do you see a black duck? | Yes. I see a black duck.

Do you see three flags? | No. I don't see three flags.

Do you see five jars? | No. I don't see five jars.

Do you see four bugs? | No. I don't see four bugs.

60

Listen. Read.

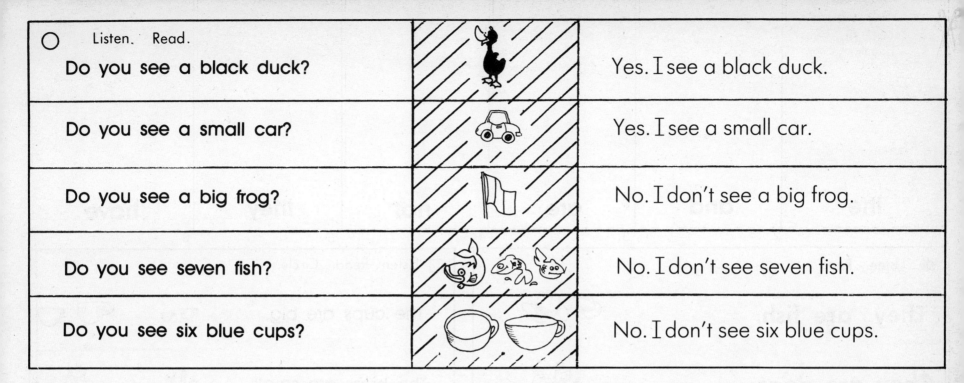

Do you see a black duck?		Yes. I see a black duck.
Do you see a small car?		Yes. I see a small car.
Do you see a big frog?		No. I don't see a big frog.
Do you see seven fish?		No. I don't see seven fish.
Do you see six blue cups?		No. I don't see six blue cups.

▲ Listen. Read. Circle.

It's a big pig.

It's not a dog.

It's a small cat.

It's not a fish.

It's not a bug.

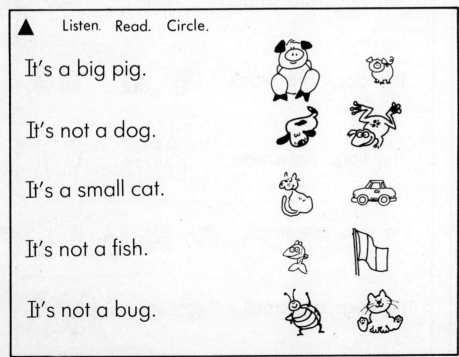

★ Listen. Read. Color.

I don't see a black duck.

I don't see a green duck.

I don't see a blue duck.

I don't see a red duck.

I see a yellow duck.

61

the	and	are	not	they	have
1	2	3	4	5	6

● Listen. Read.

They are fish.

They are dogs.

They are jars.

They are hats.

They are frogs.

They are flags.

☐ Listen. Read. Circle.

The cups are big.

The bugs are small.

The dogs are black.

The flags are small.

The cats are small.

The frogs are small.

62

The ducks are yellow and black.
The cars are red and blue.
The dogs and cats are yellow.
The jars and cups are pink.
The frogs and fish are green.

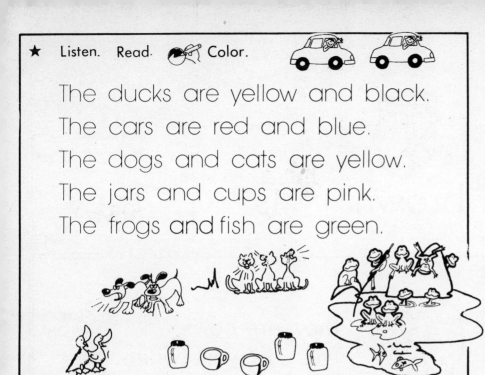

1 **They are small cats.**

2 **They are big fish.**

3 **They are black ducks.**

4 **They are small bugs.**

5 **They are big cups.**

1

They are fish.

They are big.

They are yellow.

2

They are jars.

The jars are small.

The jars are blue.

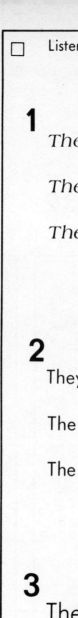

3

They are flags.

The flags are big.

The flags are blue and black.

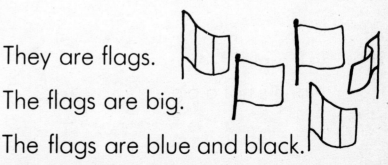

63

cow

white

The

brown

Is

They

1   2   3   4   5   6

Listen.   Read.

Is it a cow?
Yes. It's a cow.

Is it a duck?
Yes. It's a duck.

Is it a pig?
No. It's not a pig.

64

Listen.   Read.

They are cows.
The cows are white.

They are bugs.

The bugs are small.

They are dogs.

The dogs are not brown.

Listen. Read. Color.

ten = yellow   three = brown   four = white

six = blue   seven = pink   five = green

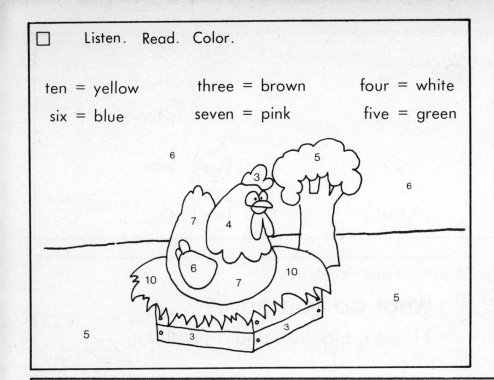

★ Listen. Read. Color.

The flags are red and yellow.

The fish are pink and green.

The beds are blue and white.

The frogs are green and brown.

○ Listen. Read. Circle.

1 **How many cows do you see?**   I see three cows.

2 **What color are the cows?**   They are black and white.

3 **What do you see?**   I see ducks.

4 **How many ducks do you see?**   I see five ducks.

5 **What color are the ducks?**   The ducks are white.

Listen.   Read.

it's   they   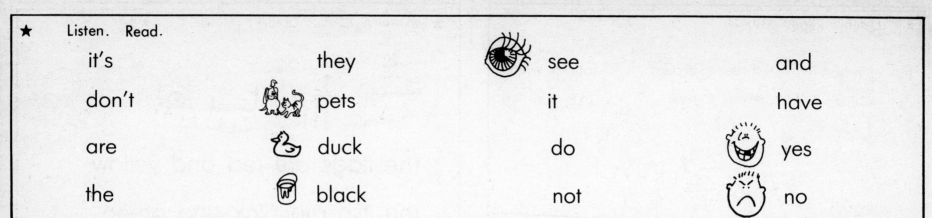 see   and

don't   pets   it   have

are   duck   do   yes

the   black   not   no

●   Listen. Read. Circle.

I see four ducks and three dogs.

I see five black cats.

I see a big car and a small jar.

I see six black pets.

66

□   Listen. Read. Circle.

What do you have?

I have a big duck and a small dog.

Do you have a cat?

No. I don't have a cat.

1 Is it a bed?

Yes. It's a bed.

No. It's not a bed.

2 Is it a cup?

Yes. It's a cup.

No. It's not a cup.

3 Is it a fish?

Yes. It's a fish.

No. It's not a fish.

4 Is it a bug?

Yes. It's a bug.

No. It's not a bug.

5 Is it a big hat?

Yes. It's a big hat.

No. It's not a big hat.

● Listen. Read. Circle. Write.

It's not a dog.

It's not a cat.

It's not big.

It's not green.

It's small.

It's a _____.

☐ Listen. Read. Circle.

I see a big cat and a duck.

I see three small bugs.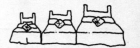

I see a dog and a flag.

I see a car and a hat.

67

★ Listen. Read. Draw.

They are ducks.

They are not cows.

The ducks are brown.

The ducks are small.

● Listen   Read. 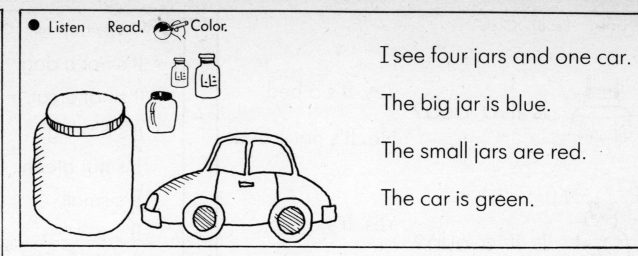 Color.

I see four jars and one car.

The big jar is blue.

The small jars are red.

The car is green.

☐ Listen.   Read.   Circle. 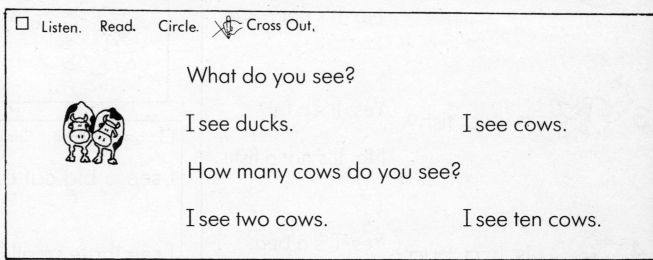 Cross Out.

What do you see?

I see ducks.   I see cows.

How many cows do you see?

I see two cows.   I see ten cows.

○ Listen   Read.   Circle.

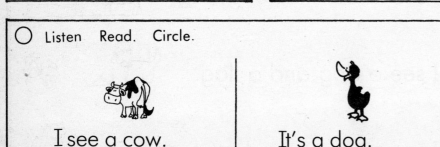

I see a cow.

I don't see a cow.

It's a dog.

It's not a dog.

▲ Listen.

two = yellow
eight = red
one = green
nine = brown

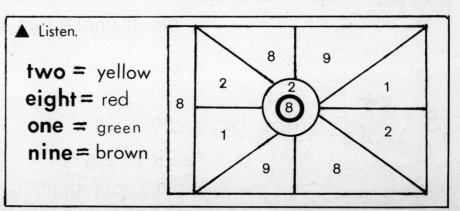

68

Where	box	in	on	bus	monkey
1	2	3	4	5	6

● Listen. Read.

1 The ball is in the box.

2 The monkey is in the box.

3 The frog is in the cup.

4 The dog is on the box.

5 The monkey is on the car.

6 The ball is on the box.

☐ Listen. Read. Color.

¹I see a monkey.
The monkey is brown.
The monkey is small.

²I see a box.
The box is not big.
The box is small.

³I see a bus.
The bus is not small.
The bus is yellow.

⁴**I see a ball.**
The ball is big.
The ball is blue and green.

69

What do you see?

I see a cat.

Where is the cat?

The cat is on the bed.

What do you see?

I see a ball.

Where is the ball?

The ball is in the box.

What do you see?

I see monkeys.

Where are the monkeys?

They are in the car.

● Listen. Read. Circle.

The monkeys are brown.   Yes   No

The monkeys are blue.   Yes   No

The monkeys are in the car.   Yes   No

The monkeys are on the car.   Yes   No

□ Listen. Read. Color.

The flags are in the blue box.

The ball is in the black box.

The red hat is in the yellow box.

		1	**2**	**9**	**8**
Do	has	one	two	nine	eight

1   2   3   4   5   6

● Listen. Read. Color.

I see two balls.
They are green.

I see nine bugs.
The bugs are red.

I see one pig.
The pig has a blue flag.

□ Listen. Read.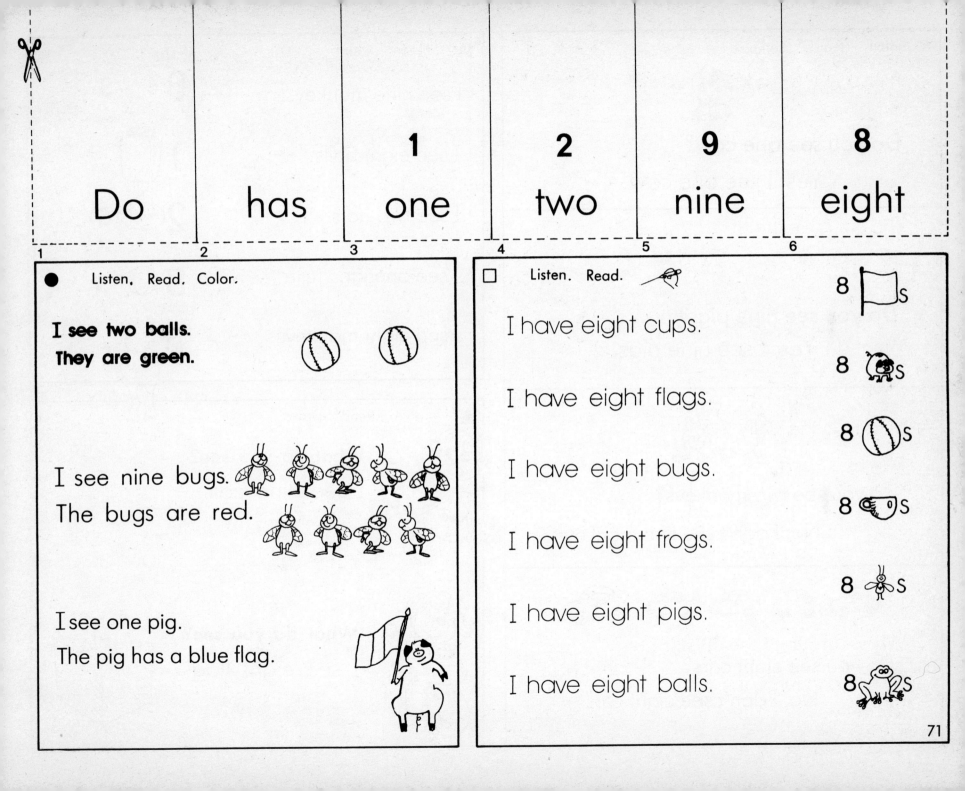

I have eight cups.   8 ⚑ s

I have eight flags.   8 🐞 s

I have eight bugs.   8 ⚾ s

I have eight frogs.   8 ☕ s

I have eight pigs.   8 🐜 s

I have eight balls.   8 🐸 s

71

★ Listen. Read. Listen.

Do you see one cow?

Yes, I see one cow.

Do you see nine pigs?

Yes, I see nine pigs.

Do you see two monkeys?

No. I don't see two monkeys.

Do you see eight cars?

No. I don't see eight cars.

72

● Listen. Read.

¹ I see nine monkeys.

8 s

² I see eight balls.

1

³ I see two hats.

2  s

⁴ I see one jar.

8 s

⁵ I see eight monkeys.

9 s

▲ Listen. Read. Draw.

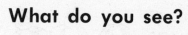

What do you see?

I see nine cats.

What do you see?

I see eight flags.

jump | swim | walk | run | can | can't

1   2   3   4   5   6

● Listen. Read.

Frogs can jump.

Frogs can swim.

Fish can't run.

Pigs can walk.

☐ Listen. Read. Circle.

1. A dog can swim.   Yes.   No.

2. A cat can walk.   Yes.   No.

3. A fish can run.   Yes.   No.

4. A cat can jump.   Yes.   No.

5. A duck can swim.   Yes.   No.

6. A cow can walk.   Yes.   No.

7. A monkey can run.   Yes.   No.

8. A fish can walk.   Yes.   No.

73

1 It can jump.
It can swim.

It is a _____.

2 They can walk.
They can run.
They can jump.
They can swim.

They are _____.

3 It can't jump.
It can't run.
It can't walk.
It can't swim.

It is a _____.

74

Are they cows?	Yes.	No.
Is it a monkey?	Yes.	No.
Are they ducks?	Yes.	No.
Is it a bus?	Yes.	No.
Are they flags?	Yes.	No.

Can ducks swim?
Yes. They can swim.
No. They can't swim.

Can flags jump?
Yes. They can jump.
No. They can't jump.

Can cows walk?
Yes. They can walk.
No. They can't walk.

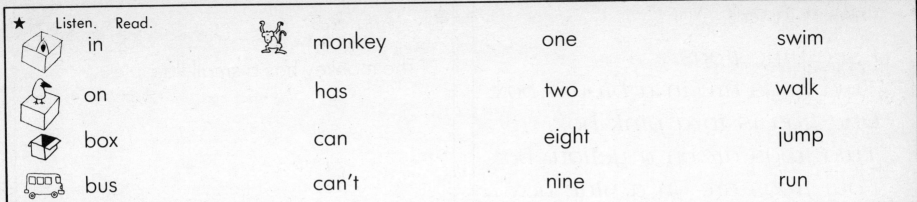

★ Listen. Read.

in	monkey	one	swim
on	has	two	walk
box	can	eight	jump
bus	can't	nine	run

● Listen. Read. Circle. Cross Out.

What do you see?

I see two monkeys.

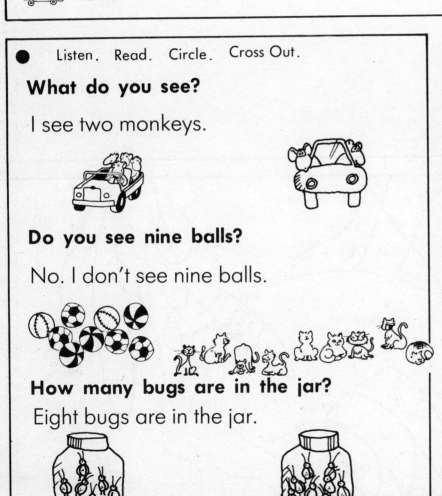

Do you see nine balls?

No. I don't see nine balls.

How many bugs are in the jar?
Eight bugs are in the jar.

□ Listen. Read. Circle. ✗ Cross Out.

A monkey <u>can   can't</u> jump.

A fish <u>can   can't</u> walk.

A frog <u>can   can't</u> run.

A dog <u>can   can't</u> swim.

A cat <u>can   can't</u> jump.

A bug <u>can   can't</u> walk.

75

I see nine frogs.
Two frogs are in a brown box.
One frog is in a pink box.
Two frogs are on a yellow box.
Four frogs are on a blue box.

The monkey has a small flag.

nine = red

two = brown

five = yellow

one = green

three = pink

six = white

four = black

eight = blue

76

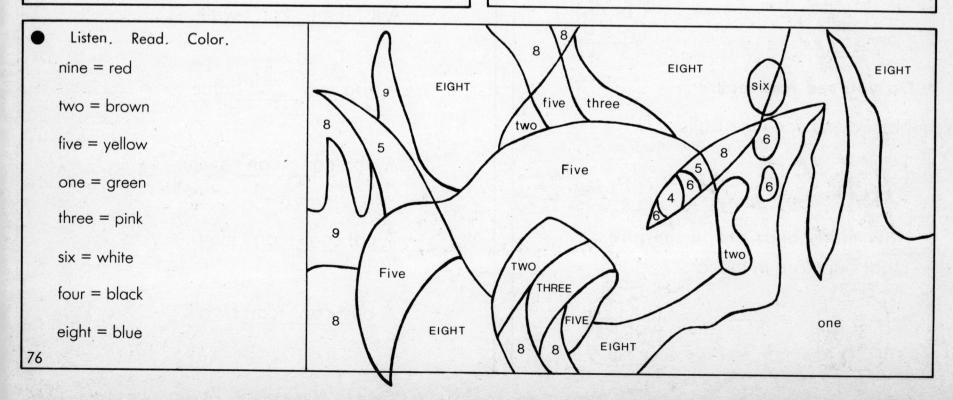

★ Listen. Read.

one= green
five= white
six= black
nine=brown
four= blue
three= pink
ten= red
eight= yellow

● Listen. Read. Circle. 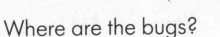 Cross Out.

Do you see seven cows?

Yes. I see seven cows.   No. I don't see seven cows.

Do you see two black ducks?

Yes. I see two black ducks.   No. I don't see two black ducks.

☐ Listen. Read. Circle. Cross Out.

Where are the bugs?

The bugs are in the box.   The bugs are on the box.

○ Listen.

1. Yes. A fish can walk.   No. A fish can't walk.

2. Yes. A frog can run.   No. A frog can't run.

3. Yes. A dog can run.   No. A dog can't run.

▲ Listen. Read. Write.

It can swim.

It can jump.

It can't walk.

It can't run.

It is a_____.

77

Listen.   Read.   Circle.

Can a duck swim?   Yes.   No.

Can a cup run?   Yes.   No.

Can a monkey jump?   Yes.   No.

Can a box walk?   Yes.   No.

Can a hat swim?   Yes.   No.

● Listen.   Read.

Draw a big dog and a cat.

Color the dog black.

Color the cat yellow.

□ Listen.   Read.   Circle.

The frogs are not in a car.

The frogs are not in a bus.

The frogs are not in a jar.

The frogs are in a box.

The frogs are big.

The frogs are green.

Color the frogs.

Are the frogs in a bus?

Yes.   No.

Are the frogs in a box?

Yes.   No.

Are the frogs black?

Yes.   No.

78

★ Listen. Read. Color.

one = yellow   five = brown

two = black   six = green

three = red   seven = blue

four = pink   eight = white

● Listen. Read. Write. wr

The Frog

Can you see the frog?
The frog is big. The frog is green.
The frog can walk.
The frog has a cup and a car.
The cup is yellow. The car is red.
A blue bug is in the car.

(?) Can the frog walk?

(.) _____

(?) What color is the bug?

(.) _____

79

1. How many frogs do you see?

_____

2. Do you see a big black hat?

_____

3. Do you see eight flags?

_____

80

I see eight black bugs

I see four big ducks.

I see two bugs.
They are in a jar.

★ Listen.　Color.　Read.　Write.

The Cats

I see ten cats.

One cat has a flag.

One cat is white.

The white cat is on the big cat.

Four cats are yellow.

Two cats are black.

Three cats are orange and brown.

1. What do you see?

2. How many cats are black?

3. How many cats are white?

4. Where is the white cat?

81

The Bugs

The red bug is in the jar.
Two green bugs are on the jar.
One blue and yellow bug is on the box.
It is a big bug.

Listen. Write.

Is the big bug in a box?

_____

Where is the red bug?

_____

Is the blue and yellow bug small?

_____

How many bugs do you see?

_____

82

The Box

The box is green.
The box is small.
The box is on the pink bed.

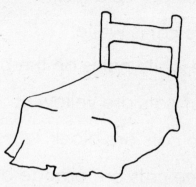

Listen. Write.

What color is the box?

_____

What color is the bed?

_____

Is the box small?

_____

Can the box jump?

_____